MOOniversity

A Student's Guide to Online Learning Environments

Jan Rune Holmevik

University of Bergen, Norway

Cynthia Haynes

University of Texas at Dallas

Allyn and Bacon

Boston ■ London ■ Toronto ■ Sydney ■ Tokyo ■ Singapore

Vice President, Humanities: *Joseph Opiela*
Editorial Assistant: *Kristen Desmond*
Editorial Production Service: *Chestnut Hill Enterprises, Inc.*
Manufacturing Buyer: *Suzanne Lareau*
Cover Administrator: *Jennifer Hart*

Copyright © 2000 by Allyn & Bacon
A Pearson Education Company
160 Gould Street
Needham Heights, MA 02494

Internet: www.abacon.com

Between the time Web site information is gathered and published, some sites may have closed. Also, the transcription of URLs can result in typographical errors. The publisher would appreciate notification where these occur so that they may be corrected in subsequent editions.

Library of Congress Cataloging-in-Publication Data

Holmevik, Jan Rune.
    MOOniversity : a student's guide to online learning environments / by Jan Rune Holmevik, Cynthia Haynes.
    ISBN 0-205-27114-6
       1. Education, Higher—Computer network resources.   2. Internet (Computer network) in education.   3. Education, Higher—Computer-assisted instruction.   I. Haynes, Cynthia (Cynthia A.)   II. Title.
LB 1044.87 .H65 2000
378.1'73'4—dc21

                                                              99-050344

Printed in the United States of America
10 9 8 7 6 5 4 3 2 1   04 03 02 01 00 99

For Johannes

CONTENTS

8   MOO Classes, Research, and Publication   125

ILLUSTRATIONS
AND TABLES

Tables

FOREWORD

Writing and Technology Series

The Series offers introductory and supplementary textbooks for use in computer-and-writing and communications classes and the Humanities in general. This series will focus on instruction in writing hypertext, on developing electronic journals and multimedia projects, on assessment and evaluation of print versus electronic culture, on Cultural Studies and the new technology, on MOOs as education sites, and on a variety of ever-growing educational concerns and challenges.

MOOniversity is the first textbook on MOOs. The authors instruct the beginner through the basics of what a MOO is and how it can be used and on to the intricacies of building virtual communities in a MOO. They also show the experienced students what the MOO can become as a site for new educational experiences. And, finally, they radically democratize the MOO by offering a new MOO core (High Wired enCore)—for all instructors to download and to develop according to their needs—and a new interface (enCore Xpress). Visit Lingua MOO at http://lingua.utdallas.edu:7000 to test ride the capabilities of the new core and interface. For a supplementary Web site for *MOOniversity*, go to http://www.abacon.com/holmevik/.

Victor J. Vitanza
Series Editor

COMPANION WEB SITE

MOOniversity Online

http://www.abacon.com/holmevik/

Writing a book about a dynamic and rapidly evolving Internet technology such as MOO presents certain challenges that we believe cannot be adequately met within the framework of a traditional print publication. Although most of the basic technological concepts and features that we talk about in this book have been around for many years and are standard in all MOOs today, there are certain systems such as, for example, enCore Xpress, that are relatively new and that are still undergoing rapid change. In order to keep up to date with the very latest technological advances in these areas, there is clearly a need for an alternate and more dynamic venue for technical information.

As teachers ourselves, we understand the need for supplemental information and support when using any textbook. We believe that students and teachers can benefit from a support network that includes the most up-to-date information as well as access to and collaboration with other students and teachers who use MOOs.

To meet these needs, we have created a companion Web site to this book. We hope that *MOOniversity* Online will serve as a useful resource for all who use educational MOOs, especially with respect to preparation, ideas for online activities, evaluation and assessment of student writing, and interaction among students in different time zones (not to mention from different cultures). Visit *MOOniversity* Online at http://www.abacon.com/holmevik/. Bookmark the site and visit it often. Let it become your personal online gateway to the exciting world of MOO!

PREFACE

Welcome to *MOOniversity* and the exciting world of MOOs!

Welcome, also, to MOOs *as* worlds of *writing*! Yes, MOOs are textual worlds that more and more writing classes (and other classes, too) are using to supplement textbook learning with interactive online learning environments. To participate, you write. To write, you think. To think, you learn. It's simple! Whether you have used MUDs or MOOs before, or have ever heard of them, this book will help you understand what they are about, and help you take advantage of the many powerful features and learning opportunities that MOO technology provides.

So what exactly is a MOO?, you may ask. Well, the word MOO is an acronym that stands for Multi-User Domain Object-Oriented (or MUD object-oriented). This may not mean much to you at this point, but be assured, it will become clear as you read the book. In short, a MOO is a computer program that allows multiple users to connect via the Internet to a shared textual world of rooms and other objects, and interact with each other and this virtual world in real time. A similar system called Internet Relay Chat (IRC) is a multiuser, multichannel chatting network that also allows people all over the Internet to talk to one another in real time. Unlike IRC, however, the MOO is a living, ever-changing textual environment. You will encounter many interesting and strange texts as you read through the sprawling landscape of text that constitutes the MOO. Not only that, you will encounter other readers with whom you can talk and become friends or colleagues. You'll be able to write new spaces in the MOOniverse where you can hang out, and where others can visit and enjoy reading what you have written about yourself and your space. If you wish, this book will even introduce you to how to program new and exciting objects in the MOO.

The power of a MOO learning environment is most aptly defined in the word *environment.* Think of a MOO as a classroom, student union, library, café, theater, laboratory, office, studio, and much, much more. Within this dynamic environment you may work individually or collectively with others. As a member of a MOO community, you may send and receive mail, participate in online events, collaborate on writing projects, record peer editing sessions, construct your own room or rooms, consult writing tutors in realtime, design your own Web pages, make presentations using graphics, sound, or video clips. The MOO really breaks the boundaries of the traditional class "room" and the typical class period. Not only this, but you will meet people from all over the United States and the world. The notion of community is expanded beyond your classroom, your university, or your country! Writing suddenly takes on new dimensions as you rely on your writing skills to communicate, navigate, and create individually and with others in the MOO.

MOOs are especially beneficial for students with learning disabilities, for the hearing-impaired, and in most cases, the visually-impaired (screen reading technologies are rapidly making text-based electronic learning much easier). Even learning a foreign language is possible in a computer-assisted language learning environment like a MOO. Of course, as exciting as this sounds, there are commands to learn, etiquette to follow, and pitfalls to avoid. And that's why we wrote *MOOniversity*.

Together, we have used MOOs for educational purposes for a number of years, both in teaching and research, as well as when we collaborate online. One of the main problems that we (and many others) have encountered when taking students to the MOO is the almost total lack of suitable information on how to use MOOs in educational environments. The situation has improved somewhat over the last few years in that there is now quite a bit of information inside MOO communities themselves (such as can be found at Lingua MOO and others). There are also quite a few Web sites around that contain information about educational uses of MOO. However, the main problem has been the lack of a good textbook on MOOs and how to use them, a problem that led us to write this book.

The fact that writing is the sole mode of communication among users at a MOO means that MOOs are especially suited for learning *about* writing, learning *by* writing, learning about others and ourselves by writing, and learning how writing in electronic environments differs from more traditional learning environments. The written word, each distinctly textual unit of meaning, evokes images, relations, connections, and emotions (among other things). Writing is a way of knowing. The MOO combines the power of the written word with the informality of the spoken context to create a rich learning environment that also holds a more important key to your learning: *you*. In a MOO you are taking part in the construction of a community, just as you do at school in your classrooms, your after-class activities, and your social communities. Your writing makes a difference in the MOO. Whether it describes a new room or contributes to a significant discussion in an online symposium, your writing *is* who you are (your self-described persona), what you think (your public and private writing), and where you hang out (your own virtual room). We call this unique combination of realtime, text, and persona a *cyphertext* (*cyber, hyper, text*). But more about that later!

Although this book is primarily written for undergraduate and graduate students taking writing courses or courses that involve the use of MOOs, it is general enough that students in others fields who want to know more about how to use a MOO will also benefit from reading it. Furthermore, teachers will also find it useful as they venture into MOOspace for the first time, as they prepare their course materials, and as a resource for connecting with other teachers who use educational MOOs. Many educators in many disciplines are prime candidates for integrating educational MOOs into their teaching, and those who do research about online learning environments, as well as those who train faculty, will find *MOOniversity* ideal for their purposes. There are many tips, shortcuts, guided questions, exercises, and visual and textual examples throughout the book. In other words, *MOOniversity* is a book that anyone interested in educational applications of MOO should read.*

In this book we make frequent mention of the High Wired enCore Educational MOO Database, also referred to as enCore, or High Wired enCore. This is a MOO database that we developed especially for educational use and that is used as the basis for building new educational MOOs (see http://lingua.utdallas.edu/encore). The enCore-specific features that we talk about in this book, for example, the enCore Xpress Web-based MOO access system, refer specifically to MOOs that are based on High Wired enCore version 2.0 or newer. To find out if the MOO you are using is an enCore-based MOO, type @*about* or @*version* while you are online. These two commands will tell you what version of enCore, if any, the MOO is based on. As you will discover, there are numerous ways to connect to a MOO, and we will take you through the options later. Just keep in mind that your first impressions during your first visit to a MOO will no doubt change rapidly as you learn. And you will learn rapidly! It is important to understand that a new and radical learning environment will perhaps be disconcerting at first, just as with any new computer program you learn. The positive effects, however, far outweigh any problems you face during the initial stages of orienting yourself in the MOO. Using a good MOO client is so important to a good first impression, not to mention ease-of-use in general. We will give you as much information, explanations, illustrations, and practice as possible. Here is a brief description of how *MOOniversity* unfolds.

In this book we have not attempted to cover every possible command or way that MOOs can possibly be used in educational environments. Because the MOO is a highly sophisticated system with hundreds of commands and ways it can be used, this would in fact be a nearly impossible task to accomplish in a textbook. Instead, we have focused on providing information that will help you get started using MOO technology and learn how MOOs are used in writing courses. You will find that this book is, at the same time, a textbook, a MOO tutorial, and a MOO reference manual; and the chapters vary in the way they deal with the subject matter. Thus, some chapters are clearly written in the style of a manual, laying out terms, giving detailed explanations and instructions for connecting, communicating, building, and other advanced features of the MOO. Other chapters focus on becoming part of a MOO community, as well as collaborating, researching, and publishing online. Throughout the book you will find discussion questions and assignments you can use to apply what you are learning.

Chapter 1 sets the stage by putting MOOs in context and talks about how this technology evolved from online multiuser games to serious educational applications. We introduce some background on virtual communities and how identity plays a role in MOOspace. Chapter 2 explains how to reach a MOO, what kind of programs you can use with MOOs, provides background on the World Wide Web (WWW) and how MOOs are integrated with the Web. Chapter 3 discusses how to use a MOO at the simplest level, such as talking to others and exploring the MOOscape. Chapter 4 deals with how to obtain a user account in a MOO, how to set various preferences, such as description, gender, and password, how to send mail to other MOO users, and much more. Chapter 5 outlines the mail, text, and verb editors you will find in the MOO, and explains how to use them.

Chapter 6 is concerned with more advanced issues, such as how to build new rooms and other objects in the MOO. Chapter 7 introduces you to object-oriented programming in the MOO. We take you through a few examples of the kind of things you can do with the MOO's most powerful design and creation feature. Chapter 8 is an introduction to class activities in MOO classrooms, and also examines how groups of students and individual students use MOOs as working environments and as home bases from which to do research. Chapter 9 moves further into research and collaboration methodologies and how collaboration takes place within classes, among several classes, and in special instances (like language learning and English as a Second Language instruction).

In addition to the nine chapters outlined above, this book also includes three handy appendices: Appendix A is a quick reference to most of the commands you can use in a MOO; Appendix B is a glossary of terms and jargon frequently used in MOOs and other online environments; and Appendix C is a list of several educational MOOs on the Internet that you can connect to and explore.

Special Symbols, Fonts, and Terms in the Text

Note that you will see commands and verbs discussed throughout the book italicized in the body of the text. When set alone in strings or with examples of dialogue, the commands and MOO responses will be in a different font, much as you will see them on the MOO. Strings of text are often referred to as the *syntax*, which simply means the correct sequence you use to type a command or something you say. Similarly, we will also use the term *argument* in the programming instructions, although this is a lengthier series of statements and expressions (see Appendix B).

Throughout this book we have used certain symbols to alert you to special features and additional information that the book provides. Here are the symbols and the explanations of what they mean.

(i)

Additional Information and Frequently Asked Questions. This is intended to supply additional or explanatory information and answers to frequently asked questions about MOOs and MOOing.

(!)

Important Point or Common Pitfall. Pay close attention whenever you see this symbol, for we are using it to point out places in the text that contain particularly important information, or that talk about common problems and pitfalls that people often experience.

(e)

High Wired enCore-Specific Feature. This symbol means that the particular feature or features we are talking about in the text can usually only be found in MOOs that are based on the High Wired enCore Educational MOO Database (see above). These features, or similar features, may also be installed in MOOs that are not based on enCore, but to find out whether they are, you need to ask the MOO's administrators.

(?)

Exercises and Class Activities. At the end of each chapter, we have designed a few exercises and topics for class discussion that will help you learn some of the more important things that we have discussed in that chapter. Most of these activities require you to be online and logged on to a MOO.

As we wrote this book we wanted to convey the kind of enjoyment and playfulness that comes from using MOOs. We believe that learning happens well when students are enjoying the learning process and are motivated by *it* as much as by the results they hope to achieve. Thus, we believe that learning in MOO environments is a new way of learning that enhances the traditional composition classroom where we have been taught that learning to write usually takes place.

It is our hope that this book will lead to a wider adoption of MOO technology in schools and universities, so that as many students as possible can have the opportunity to experience for themselves what a wonderful learning experience MOOing can be. Enjoy this book and enjoy your MOOing experiences that lie ahead.

Acknowledgments

We want to express our deepest thanks to Victor J. Vitanza for the opportunity to publish this book, and for his unfailing support throughout this project. We would also like to thank the reviewers who provided encouragement and many valuable suggestions. Thanks also to Joe Opiela and the team at Allyn & Bacon for having faith in our project. We must also extend our gratitude to Britt Høyland and the students in Cynthia's "Electronic Expression" class (1998), who all contributed feedback on early drafts of the manuscript.

The MOO community is an especially generous group of people, and our work has been much inspired by the efforts of many who went before us and sustained us along the way. Thus, we want to extend our heartfelt gratitude to Espen Aarseth, Jorge Barrios, Mark Blanchard, Amy Bruckman, Juli Burk, Eric Crump, Pavel Curtis, Isabel Danforth, D. Diane Davis, Michael Day, Tari Fanderclai, Traci Gardner, Gustavo Glusman, Michael Joyce, Judi Kirkpatrick, Beth Kolko, Ken Schweller, Greg Siering, Sindre Sørensen, Sherry Turkle, Deanna Wilkes-Gibbs, and many others.

The following reviewers made timely and helpful suggestions: Michael Day, Northern Illinois University; Roxanne Mountford, University of Arizona; and Peter Sands, University of Wisconsin–Milwaukee.

Finally, we are indebted to the University of Bergen, Norway and the University of Texas at Dallas for institutional and professional support.

Notes

*For more information about composition on the Internet, see Allyn & Bacon's Composition Web site located on the WWW at:

http://www.abacon.com/compsite/index.html

ABOUT THE AUTHORS

Jan Rune Holmevik is a visiting assistant professor and doctoral candidate in the Department of Humanistic Informatics at the University of Bergen, Norway. He holds a degree in the history of science and technology from the University of Trondheim, Norway, 1994. He is coeditor of *High Wired: On the Design, Use and Theory of Educational MOOs*, Ann Arbor: University of Michigan Press, 1998, with Dr. Cynthia Haynes of the University of Texas at Dallas (UTD). His Master of Arts thesis, *Educating the Machine: A Study in the History of Computing and the Construction of the SIMULA Programming Languages*, was published by the Center for Technology and Society, Trondheim, Norway in 1994. His other publications on the history of computing and science policy have appeared in journals such as *Annals of the History of Computing, Forskningspolitikk,* and *Kairos.* With Cynthia Haynes, Holmevik is cofounder and administrator of Lingua MOO (1995), a synchronous Internet-based learning environment hosted by UTD. Holmevik is also the principal architect and maintainer of The High Wired enCore, the first publicly available educational MOO core database, and the author of enCore Xpress, a Web-based MOO access system designed to make MOOs more accessible and easier to use.

Cynthia Haynes is Assistant Professor in the School of Arts & Humanities and Director of Rhetoric and Writing at the University of Texas at Dallas where she teaches graduate and undergraduate rhetoric, composition, and electronic pedagogy courses. Her publications have appeared in *Pre/Text, Composition Studies, Keywords in Composition, St. Martin's Guide to Tutoring Writing, Works & Days, The Writing Center Journal, Kairos,* and *Computers, Writing, Rhetoric, and Literature.* She is coeditor of *Pre/Text: Electra(Lite),* and, with Jan Rune Holmevik, she is cofounder of Lingua MOO. With Jan Rune Holmevik, Dr. Haynes is coeditor of *High Wired: On the Design, Use and Theory of Educational MOOs,* published by University of Michigan Press. Her interests in rhetorical delivery and electronic scholarship spawned the C-FEST series of online real-time meetings at Lingua MOO where these issues are debated year-round. She is currently at work on her book, *Beta Rhetoric: Releasing Ethos 3.0b.*

1 MOOs in Context

Background and History: From Multi-User Games to Educational MOOs

Over the past ten to fifteen years MUDs have been among the most popular Internet applications. The word MUD, funny as it may seem, is really an acronym for Multi-User Dungeon, or, as many prefer to call it, Multi-User Domain. In this book we focus on a particular strain of MUD called MOO (Multi-User Domain, Object-Oriented), that has recently become particularly popular in educational environments. In its simplest form, a MUD or MOO is a computer program that allows people from all over the world to connect via the Internet to a text-based virtual world where they can interact with each other and the virtual world that is simulated by the MOO system. The textual universe of the MOO resides on a server machine that can be located anywhere in the world, and players typically use a client program like Telnet, for example, to connect to the MOO via computer networks such as the Internet.

MUDs and MOOs are artifacts of the Hacker Culture, and their history rests on two principal foundations. One is the Hacker Ethic; the other is the adventure computer game. In his book, *Hackers: Heroes of the Computer Revolution* (1984), Steven Levy has examined the Hacker Culture from its origins at Massachusetts Institute of Technology (MIT) in the late 1950s until the mid-1980s. The cornerstone of this culture, he contends, is the Hacker Ethic. For the purpose of this chapter we will limit ourselves to two aspects of this ethic that have had a profound bearing on the history of MUDs: free access to information and the perfection of systems.

To hack in computing terms means to take an existing computer program and modify it to suit one's own needs and preferences. At the time when computers were far less powerful than they are today, writing programs that would make the most out of the limited computer resources at hand were very important. For the early hackers at MIT, the purpose of hacking was to make existing programs smaller and more efficient. The motive for doing this was often to impress one's friends or peers; hence, listings of computer code were circulated freely for others to read, to learn from, and to be impressed by. When Roy Trubshaw and Richard Bartle of Essex University in the United Kingdom wrote the first MUD in 1979, they made all the source code available for others to use and improve on. As a result, MUDs could soon be found at other universities both in the UK and other countries.

```
You are standing at the end of a road before a small brick
building. Around you is a forest. A small stream flows out
of the building and down a gully.
```

The themes of the early MUDs were usually inspired by the now-classic adventure games, *Adventure* and *Zork*. Typically you would assume the role of a rogue seeking treasure and adventure in some vast and dangerous dungeon. One important reason for the choice of dungeons as a setting for these games was the role-playing system, *Dungeons & Dragons*, which became widespread and highly popular among (predominantly male) college students in the 1970s.

Because of the freely available MUD code, and the hacker ideal of perfecting systems, by 1990 a great number of MUDs with funny names, LPMUD, AberMUD, MUCK, MUSH, and MOO, could be found on the Internet. Most of these were built and inhabited by college students. Some of these so-called MUDDers were hackers (also known as wizards) who maintained and developed the systems, but the majority were players who came to play the game or to chat. In most of these new MUDs the dungeons and dragons theme prevailed and was as popular as ever before, but a new trend was also emerging.

In 1989, a graduate student at Carnegie Mellon University, James Aspnes, wrote a MUD he called TinyMUD. It was a typical hack, written in one weekend. In contrast to other MUDs that could only be modified by wizards with special programming privileges, the TinyMUD was user-extendable, which meant that anyone could add to it. The design of the MUD architecture was no longer a privilege for the wizards only. In the TinyMUD, anyone with an account on the system could build new locations and objects and describe them as s/he wished.

Around 1990, the user-extendable philosophy of the TinyMUD was taken one step further when Stephen White, and later Pavel Curtis, developed the MOO system with a host of new and powerful tools that were designed to make it easy for people to help build the virtual MOO world. Most often people would use metaphors from their familiar surroundings to describe the places they created in the MOO. The reason for this may have been a desire to bring some familiarity to the strange new surroundings of the MOO. Most people who visit a MUD or a MOO for the first time feel a little intimidated by the overload of text, and it is easy to lose track of where you are in the nonphysical MOOspace. By using commonly known metaphors like rooms or dungeon caves, however, the users get a sense of physical surroundings that help in navigating the MOOscape. At LambdaMOO, the biggest and most popular MOO on the Internet at the time of this writing (1998), you enter cyberspace through a linen closet. Once you step out of this closet you find yourself in the welcoming and familiar surroundings of a living room where you might find a chair you can relax in and, of course, other players to talk to. In fact, when Pavel Curtis first built LambdaMOO, he purposely designed it based on the layout of his own home.[1]

Educational MOOs

Some of the early visitors to LambdaMOO realized that the MOO technology also had a great potential for professional purposes. Amy Bruckman, then a graduate student of MIT's Media Lab, envisioned MOO as a virtual meeting place for media researchers, and in 1992 she started MediaMOO, which has had an enormous significance for the professionalization of MOO technology. It demonstrated that a technology that had predominantly been used for gaming and online chat purposes could be put to serious and productive use. Second, it became an important meeting place for academics and others curious about this technology and what it could be used for. Here you see the TV Studio at MediaMOO where we first met and conceived the idea for creating our own MOO:

```
┌──────────────────────── mediamoo.media.mit.edu:8888 (1) ──────────────────────┐
│ @go MEdiaMOO TV Studio                                                         │
│ MediaMOO TV Studio                                                             │
│ WELCOME to the MMTV Studio.   If there's any equipment you need just 'activate │
│   Robbie' and ask him for it!                                                  │
│       _____            |  N  |_____         │
│      |                           |           |     |                  |        │
│      |                           |           | TVs    VCRs    TAPES   CAMERAS| │
│      |                           |           | SLIDE PROJECTORS         |      │
│      |                           |           | CONVERSATIONAL BOTS      |      │
│      |                           |           |                          |      │
│      |     Tape Editing Room     W           <<  MMTV STUDIO >>         |      │
│      |                           |  _                                   |      │
│      |                           | |_____          \O/       |      │
│      |                           | | Tape Library |  <> ROBBIE          |      │
│      |_____|_|_____|___/_____|      │
│                                                                                │
│ Obvious exits: west to Tape Editing Room and N to West Media Ave.              │
│ You see Broadcaster, VAX 11/780, Robbie, broadcast monitor, Tape Library, MediaM│
│ OO TV Helicopter, and PLAQUE here.                                             │
│ Robbie says, "[to Cyn] I like mediaMOO a lot, its fun to explore and learn new t│
│ hings."                                                                         │
└────────────────────────────────────────────────────────────────────────────────┘
```

FIGURE 1.1   MediaMOO TV Studio

After the establishment of MediaMOO, other professionally oriented MOOs began to appear. BioMOO, founded in 1993 by Gustavo Glusman and Jaime Prilusky of the Weizmann Institute of Science in Israel, was built as a meeting place for biologists. About the same time, Jeanne MacWhorter, a social worker, had the idea of starting a MOO for people of her profession. As she began work on this project, however, she realized that it would be more fruitful to incorporate other disciplines, and thus was born Diversity University, the largest multidisciplinary MOO on the Internet today.

With MediaMOO, BioMOO, AstroVR, CollegeTown, and other professional MOOs of the first generation, teachers could not bring their classes online. Recently, however, MOOs with more explicit educational missions have appeared, where teachers are welcome to bring their students online. Here they explore the potential of this technology for a host of applications, such as online writing centers, electronic classrooms, hypertextual writing spaces, Net-based collaborative environments, or complete cyberspace-based campuses, as Diversity University is today.

Communities on the Internet

While there are numerous fascinating communities such as LambdaMOO in the MUD/MOO world, it is necessary to understand that there are behavior expectations in these communities just as there are in "real-life" communities. You may hear people refer to online communities as "virtual communities" in order to distinguish them from "real-life" (or RL) communities, and we will refer to them this way for the purpose of making that distinction. However, it's important to remember that virtual communities are just as "real" as real communities. That is, they are made up of real people just like you, and real communities involve social interaction.

Basically all multi-user synchronous environments are socially constructed spaces. They are more often than not created by many people and populated by many users. However, educational MOOs tend to distinguish themselves from the more socially oriented MOOs in several ways. First, educational MOOs are created to provide new and innovative ways for students to learn, but learning is best achieved with few distractions. Social MOOs tend to be a bit more chaotic and unfocused. It is sometime difficult to hold a conversation at a social MOO without unwelcome interruptions, whereas it is safe to assume that an educational MOO posts the same kind of etiquette rules you can expect on any campus, in any classroom. Second, learning requires accessibility to resources often unavailable on social MOOs. For example, an educational MOO will usually contain specially programmed classrooms, blackboards, research tools, and many more items created to enhance the learning experience. Finally, educational MOOs are more likely to be populated by students just like you. Remember: teachers and MOO administrators are working to provide you with a safe, enjoyable, and productive learning environment, and one of the best parts about meeting at a MOO is that you can meet other students from around the world, and in some cases you can even collaborate with them on projects of your own design. We will say more about these possibilities in Chapter 9.

Now that you have a feel for how MOOs have evolved in recent years and the various types of MOOs there are, it's time to focus on some general guidelines for what to expect in MOOspace. The first thing you need to know is that you can believe about 50% of what you hear about cyberspace and virtual communities. The popular media tend to focus on the sensational and negative aspects of "chat rooms." To be sure, there are countless spaces on the Internet in which you may interact with others online in real time. Unfortunately, the media have sensationalized "chat rooms" by reporting primarily the negative encounters that sometimes occur, whether those involve mindless "chat," harassment, or sexual predators looking for victims. Less often the media publish stories about the thousands of people who meet online to experience encouragement in difficult times, information about medical problems, or like-minded groups seeking to connect as explained in the following MOOmail we received from Jasminko, a player at Lingua MOO who is from Croatia:

```
Date: Sat Nov 16 10:53:10 1996 CST
From: Jasminko (#1381)
To: Jan (#2), Jasminko (#1381), and Cynthia (#84)
Subject: MOO demo & conference

Hello friends!

Once again, I shall call upon you.:-) I'm doing a demo about
MOOs at a conference here in Zagreb. It would be great if I
could have some ppl connect real-time to the MOO and play-out
a more/less prepared scenario. Friday, November 22, 2-3pm
EDT/EST, 18-19 CET/MET. The conference is on "Europe of
Cultures", and the demo is part of my presentation of
CulturelinkMOO project under theme3 "cooperative networking
& multicultural communication.... Ideally, the demo should
paint a picture, or at least give an idea, of how a MOO
should/could/will contribute/enhance the functioning of
Culturelink (network of networks of institutions&individuals
in the field of culture) by becoming its communication
medium.
```

We can attest to the fact that there are many more positive encounters in real-time multi-user Internet environments than there are negative ones.

Thus, it is a challenge to sort through the hype, but well worth the trouble once you do. To help you get a handle on what is at stake in the tendency of the media to highlight the negative, there are some issues about identity you need to understand before you "set foot" in a MOO.

Identity

One of the most appealing aspects of interacting in cyberspace is the ability to be whatever and whoever you want to be. Like most freedoms, however, this has its upside and downside. For example, at our MOO, Lingua MOO, it is not uncommon for a player to mistake us for a computer program. In fact, one time a whole fourth grade class would simply not believe that Jan Rune Holmevik was a real person! The students who visited Lingua that day thought he was a robot, or "bot" as they are called on MOOs. To convince them that he was real, Jan Rune volunteered to mail them a *real* postcard from Norway through the mail just to prove his existence! They agreed and gave him their addresses, to which he mailed the card.

Many MOO users feel like exploring the MOOscape under an assumed name. While it is fun to experiment with who you are by identifying and describing yourself in new and creative ways, identity is a tricky business. The key is to remember that you possess only some control over how others perceive you in cyberspace. In other words, people you meet on a MOO will be limited to the textual cues they read about you (as well as the text you "say" and "emote"), not the visual cues that come with meeting you face-to-face (F2F). Textual cues can be divided into four categories: player's name, player's gender, player's description, and player's conversation and actions.

Although your teacher may require you to use your given name when online, many educational MOOs require students to log on as guest players, and you are not allowed to choose the name assigned to you. You might be connected as "Purple-Guest" or "Poodle-Guest." Other MOOs may allow all guests (students and all other users) to use their own name or choose a name they prefer.

In the first case, you are basically anonymous. If you are allowed to choose your own name, you are not anonymous. Sometimes, however, even when you are allowed to choose your own name, there may already be a player by that name, in which case you will be asked to pick another name. Sometimes people just add their last name initial (i.e., Cynthia-H). Other times, players choose a nickname (i.e., Cindy), or a completely different name altogether. Let's say that you want to call yourself "Jasmine" or "Pepper." Suddenly you realize that your identity is a mask not unlike a "real" mask you might wear to a costume party. The same holds true for "Purple-

Guest"; your identity is a mystery to all who encounter you. Names are important identifiers in our culture. A name "says" something about us even before we say something about ourselves.

In short, if you are given a choice, you would be wise to give it some thought. How others perceive you is often determined to some degree by the name they see. If you log on as "skullcruncher," people will have a specific impression of your persona. Your ethos (credibility) evokes an image of some violent Neanderthal looking for virtual skulls to crunch. If you are playing some adventure game in a video arcade, that might be an appropriate persona to adopt. On an educational MOO, it is not. Keep in mind that you are visible in any number of ways to any number of people whenever you are logged on. You cannot assume that just because you are talking to someone in your own room, or are alone in some public part of the MOO, that no one can "see" you. Chances are, however, that people to whom you would not normally represent yourself as a skullcruncher are just as likely to log on as those you would interact with in an adventure hack-and-slay MUD. This is especially true in an educational MOO.

Imagine what the Deputy Minister of Croatia would think if, for his first MOO experience, he logged on to Lingua MOO while "skullcruncher" was online. Imagine how this might influence his decision to grant the Culture Link project funds and technical support. Because of the newness of such spaces as viable learning environments, and because of the media attention to the negative aspects of real-time teletechnologies like MOOs, and "chat rooms" in general, it is sometimes very difficult to persuade administrators and other kinds of officials that MOOs have the potential to be powerful teaching tools as well as significant alternative modes of communication between people in remote locations. In other words, the MOO is a community made up of real people doing real work. A certain amount of respect and etiquette goes a long way toward building a community like that on an educational MOO.[2]

Not only is it important to consider what name you choose, but there are other factors that make being anonymous advantageous and disadvantageous. When you are anonymous (whether you are Purple-Guest or Jasmine), you are subject to misunderstandings at the very least and harassment at the worst. Anonymity can create the conditions for unwanted verbal abuse. But it is also a powerful creative tool. That is, sometimes being anonymous allows you the freedom to experiment, to be creative, when you otherwise might not feel free to be. It may not occur to you to present yourself online as other than who you are, but keep in mind that one of the best aspects about being online is the freedom to voice your opinion in a relatively safe space. Some of you may feel that using another name or describing yourself differently makes you feel more inclined to speak up. The downside is that if everyone has this ability, you can be sure someone is bound to abuse it at some point. In other words, anonymity can work in your favor or not, as the case may be.

Many educational and professional MOOs recognize the importance of fostering a creative and playful learning environment, while at the same time protecting their users from potential harassment. In these MOOs, you may be anonymous only to some extent. That is, you may be allowed to choose a name other than your real name, but in order to have a player account you must provide your real name and real e-mail address. This information is accessible to all other players at any time through a command like *@whois* followed by the player-name.

After you choose the name with which you will log in, two of the first preferences you should set are your gender and a description of yourself. Again, these are "textual cues" that other players use to find out who you are and what you are like. Before you set your gender, you might want to look at the various gender options available by typing *@gender*. Once you have set your gender, you should write a brief description of yourself. You will find out more about both of these in Chapter 4, but at this point you should be thinking about how you want to describe yourself in text. Of course your gender setting may determine some of the nature of your description, though it doesn't have to. In general, use your imagination, but exercise good taste. Ask yourself what kind of image you want to evoke when others *look* at you. Write it in such a way that it paints a portrait of you in text. Here is an example of a brief player description:

```
look Truthseeker
A woman stands tall before you, all 5'8 of her. She is young
but her eyes show more wisdom than her years would suggest
and her youthful face gives clues that her family line has
always looked younger than their years. Long, wavy, brown-
auburn hair falls down to her waist and several braids are
tucked among the loose strands decorated with feathers and
amber beads. Her honey gold skin is always complemented by
her choice of clothing. The dragon-shaped jade amulet around
her neck is elegant in its simplicity and she never takes it
off. The same type of jade forms a fine looking bracelet at
her right wrist; it is an amalgam of dragons, firelizards,
dolphins and runnerbeasts.
```

Finally, just as you are represented in text through your name, gender, and description, other players will get their fullest sense about you by what you say and do. The text you write takes several forms, some of which will be discussed in later chapters, but for now let's focus on talking and emoting. During your first visit to a MOO, your teacher will take you through the basic commands for talking and emoting (see Chapter 3 for more details), or she will ask you to explore how to do this on your own. In either case, you should remember some important things about how text affects people who have nothing else with which to understand one another.

- Write in short bursts of text. Lengthy sentences or paragraphs of text are difficult to read while lots of other text is causing your screen to scroll up as the conversation continues. If you want to write in snippets, using an ellipsis (…) before you hit Enter tells the others in the room that you still have more to say.
- Be careful about using all capital letters. It has the effect of SHOUTING!
- Keep in mind that if you are being funny or ironic, unless you accompany what you say with a textual emote (like smiling or rolling your eyes), the other players may not get the joke. They might even take offense.
- Try to direct your talk to specific people when you are not addressing the whole group (use the "stage talk" feature). This cuts down on the confusion when lots of people are talking in the same room.
- If you want to say something to another player better said in private, and you are in a group, *please* page or whisper to that player. But *be careful* about accidentally saying to the whole room what you meant to say as a page to one player. This has caused many an embarassing moment.

Exercise caution and common sense when deciding who you are and how you want to represent yourself in the MOO. Make sure that you think carefully about how you want others to perceive you. Similarly, it is very important to understand that if you take advantange of being anonymous and use an offensive name and engage in offensive behavior, your privileges in the MOO community could be revoked. A MOO is no different from any campus and classroom environment in that respect. A good rule of thumb is to be considerate of others and do not behave in ways you would not in a "real" classroom.

NOTES

1. The section on the history of MUDs and MOOs also appears in part in Haynes, Holmevik, Kolko, and Vitanza's "MOOs, Anarchitexture, towards a New Threshold," in *The Emerging CyberCulture: Literacy, Paradigm, and Paradox,* eds. Stephanie Gibson and Ollie Oviedo. Reprinted here with permission from Hampton Press.

2. For a good selection of MOO-related articles and Web sites, some of which deal with virtual communities and identity issues like those discussed in this chapter, see the Lingua MOO Archive and Resource page located on the WWW at:

   http://lingua.utdallas.edu/archive.html

   Additional articles about MUDs and MOOs can be found in Victor Vitanza's *Cyber-Reader* (Allyn & Bacon, 1998). To get a preview of the book and related links, go to:

   http://www.abacon.com/~cyber/

CLASS DISCUSSION

1. Group discussion topic: Discuss your experiences in other kinds of chat spaces (even the phone can be construed as a chat space) or adventure games (or video games) and compare with other students in your class.

2. As your class prepares for its first MOO session, it would be helpful to discuss some of the key issues about "virtual communities" outlined in this chapter. Questions to consider for discussion:

   - What is "virtuality" and how do you distinguish it from "reality," or do you?
   - How do you feel about learning in relation to the element of "play" versus seriousness?
   - What are the advantages and disadvantages of being anonymous or "real" in a MOO? How do you define *identity* in this regard?

3. List as many of the typical protocols for behavior in a traditional RL classroom as you can. Now, do the same for a virtual classroom. What similarities and differences do you note? If you added protocols for virtual space that you did not have for traditional classroom spaces, what are they? If you omitted certain things from your virtual classroom list, what are they?

EXERCISES

Start a MOO notebook in which you keep notes and document (in a journal style) your introduction to MOOing with *MOOniversity*. Keep your notebook organized (and private, especially if you keep your passwords there). Here are some suggestions for various sections of your notebook:

- A list of MOOs and their Internet addresses
- Your MOO character user name for each MOO account you have (It is not a good idea to write your password down because it could be read by others, but if you decide to do so in your MOO notebook, then be sure that your notebook is secure at all times.)
- Special features and themes you note in the MOO

- Objects and commands you need to refer to frequently (see Appendix A for a helpful list)
- Objects you own and their object numbers
- Special feature objects for customized communication and other actions
- WWW sites for further research on MOOs
- Upcoming MOO events you would like to attend
- Lists of other MOO players you meet and how to contact them
- Help texts you may want to print out and attach
- Building policies for different MOOs
- InMOO newsgroups you want to subscribe to
- Drafts of various descriptions for your character and objects
- Online Learning Record (see Chapter 8)
- Ideas for MOO projects and project schedules

2 Fly Me to the MOO[1]

MOO Clients

MOOs are quite different from most other computer software you have probably used. One reason is that they do not reside on the hard disk of your computer like, for example, your word processing program typically does. Instead, MOOs reside on remote computers that may be physically located as far away as the other side of the world. To reach a MOO, therefore, you need to use a program called a *MOO client.* Imagine the MOO client program as a bridge across the Internet that connects your computer with the computer that runs the MOO. Once you have established a connection to the MOO, there will be a lot of "traffic" across this bridge carrying information from the MOO to you and vice versa.

The simplest of all such client programs is called *Telnet,* which is available through almost all university UNIX accounts, and on most personal computer systems as well. This means that, if you have access to the Internet, you have access to basically all the MOOs there are. Although Telnet is really all you need to use a MOO, we recommend instead that you use a more sophisticated client program. The main reason is that Telnet doesn't separate what you type in from what others in the MOO say and do, and this often results in interruptions while you type. Namely, the text you type will frequently get broken up by text that the MOO sends back to you (see Chapter 3 for another alternative, called an *output delimiter,* used in some MOOs). Needless to say, this can be very frustrating and confusing for new MOO users. The best way to deal with the problem is to get a good MOO client that has the capability to separate what you type to the MOO from what the MOO sends back to you. In most cases, this means a client program that has a split window with an input area and an output area as shown in Figures 2.1, 2.2, and 2.3.

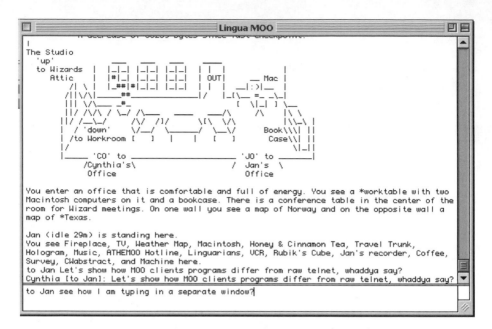

FIGURE 2.1   Input and Output Window Using MUDDweller Client (Mac only)

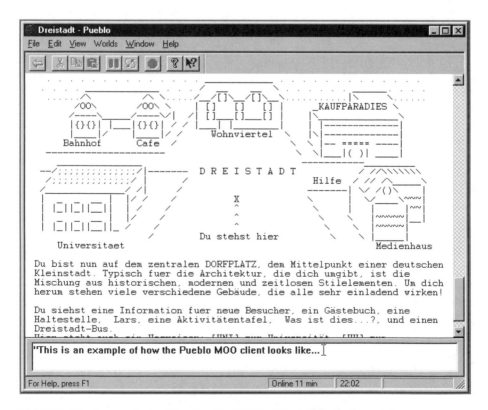

FIGURE 2.2   Screenshot of the Pueblo MOO Client (Windows only)

14

Figure 2.3 shows how the window looks when you use a raw Telnet program:

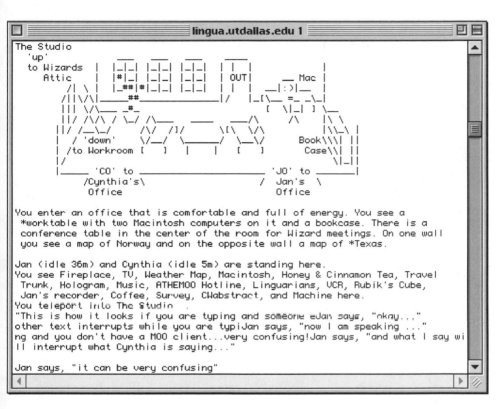

FIGURE 2.3   Input and Output in the Same Window Using NCSA Telnet (Windows and Mac)

(i)

Here are a few client programs that you can use with MOOs[2].

- Macintosh
  MacMOOSE:
  http://www.cc.gatech.edu/fac/Amy.Bruckman/MacMOOSE/
  MUDDweller: ftp://mac.archive.umich.edu:/mac/util/comm
- UNIX
  TinyFugue:ftp://ftp.math.okstate.edu:/pub/muds/clients/UnixClients

- Microsoft Windows
  MudWin: ftp://ftp.microserve.com/pub/msdos/winsock/
  Pueblo: http://www.chaco.com/pueblo/

Web-Based MOO Access and Client Systems

An alternative to using a local MOO client program like those listed above is to use what we call a Web-based access system. The World Wide Web (WWW) was invented around 1990 as a vehicle for researchers to share information using the powerful and versatile information infrastructure provided by the Internet. It quickly became very popular because of the way it enabled people to publish cheaply and easily hypertextual and multimedia rich information with a potential for reaching millions of people worldwide.

With the advent of the World Wide Web, MOO programmers began to research how this new Internet technology could be used as a framework for bringing multimedia content to the traditional text-based world of MOOs. Among the first of these efforts were Jays House MOOs WWW system, and Sensemedia's WOO system (WOO stands for WWW + MOO). Since the mid-1990s a host of such Web-based access systems has been developed, among them the BioGate System (by BioGate Partners Gustavo Glusman, Eric Mercer, and others), the E_MOO Web System, and enCore Xpress, which is the one we will discuss specifically in this book.

All these are platform-independent, Web-distributed systems that you use via your Web browser. What is important to remember is that you can only use them in MOOs where they have been installed. If your MOO does not provide a Web-based access system, such as the ones mentioned above, your only option is to use a traditional client.

The main strength of the Web-based access systems is that they are generally easier to use than traditional MOO clients, and they provide a feature-rich hypertextual multimedia interface to the MOO where images, audio, and video (and more) can be closely integrated elements of the MOO experience. On the other hand, because of the bandwidth demand of multimedia content that they deliver, Web-based access systems usually require faster computers and higher-speed Internet connections than do the traditional text-only clients.

Figure 2.4 shows an example of how multimedia content, such as a Quick-Time Movie, can be experienced in the MOO using a Web-based access system.

Noninteractive MOO Browsing

MOOs that have a Web-based access system like BioGate (Fig. 2.5) or enCore Xpress usually also provide a way for users to explore the MOOscape in a

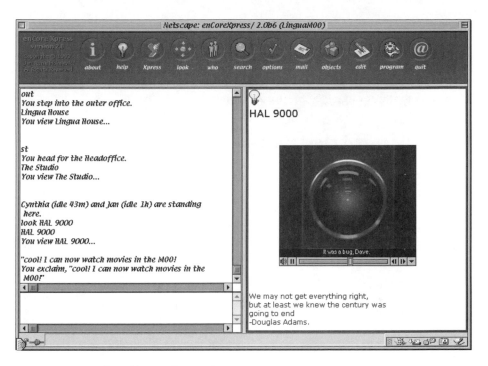

FIGURE 2.4 enCore Xpress Screenshot

FIGURE 2.5 BioGate Screenshot

noninteractive browsing mode. To access a MOO in this mode, you must point your Web browser to an *entry point,* where you should find a link to the MOO's Web login page (see Figure 2.10 below).

IP Numbers and Domain Names

Every computer on the Internet has its own unique identification number, also known as its IP number. This is a series of digits separated by dots that shows where in the world the machine is located. A typical IP number looks like this:

129.110.16.13

Because IP numbers can be hard to remember, you can also refer to a machine by its *domain name.* Domain names are much easier to remember and give us a lot of useful information at a glance. The domain name that corresponds to the IP number above is:

lingua.utdallas.edu

This domain name tells us that the machine is called lingua, that it can be found at the University of Texas at Dallas (UTD), and that UTD is located in the United States. Domain names and IP numbers, in other words, can be thought of as a particular computer's address on the information superhighway. The domain name or IP number is the address to the machine on which the MOO resides, and in order to connect to it, you must enter this informa-

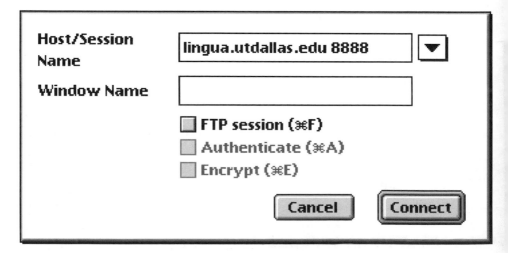

FIGURE 2.6   NCSA Telnet Connect Session Window

tion into your client program. Figure 2.6 shows what appears on the screen when you open a session with NCSA Telnet.

Network Ports

Because a computer may run many other programs, like a WWW server or FTP server in addition to the MOO, you also need to tell your client program which *port* to connect to. Think of the port number as a street address that tells your client program which house to enter. Most educational MOOs use the port numbers 7777 or 8888, as shown in Figure 2.7, but other port numbers are also being used.

If you are logging in from your UNIX account at school using Telnet (among MOO veterans often referred to as *raw telnet* because of its lack of layout features), Figure 2.8 shows what you would type to connect to Lingua MOO:

telnet lingua.utdallas.edu 8888

If you are using a more sophisticated client program, which we strongly encourage you to do, you will have to enter the domain name and port information into your client program before you can connect. Pueblo from Chaco Communications is a popular MOO client for the Windows platform. In this program, you create your own list of MOOs that you visit often, called a *world list* (see Figure 2.9). Once you have entered and stored connect information, such as the MOO domain name and port number, and user name and password, in your world list, you can later simply click on the MOO you want to visit in order to connect.

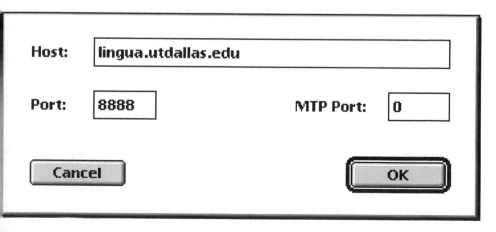

FIGURE 2.7   MUDDweller Connect Session Window

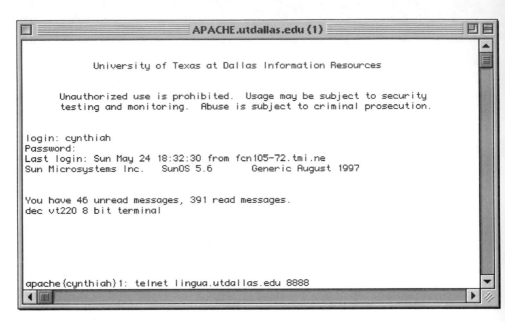

```
┌──────────────────────────────────────────────────────────────────────────┐
│ □          ════════ APACHE.utdallas.edu (1) ════════          ▣ ▤        │
├──────────────────────────────────────────────────────────────────────────┤
│                                                                         ▲ │
│                                                                         ▤ │
│         University of Texas at Dallas Information Resources              │
│                                                                          │
│      Unauthorized use is prohibited.  Usage may be subject to security   │
│      testing and monitoring.  Abuse is subject to criminal prosecution.  │
│                                                                          │
│                                                                          │
│  login: cynthiah                                                         │
│  Password:                                                               │
│  Last login: Sun May 24 18:32:30 from fcn105-72.tmi.ne                   │
│  Sun Microsystems Inc.   SunOS 5.6        Generic August 1997            │
│                                                                          │
│                                                                          │
│  You have 46 unread messages, 391 read messages.                         │
│  dec vt220 8 bit terminal                                                │
│                                                                          │
│                                                                          │
│                                                                          │
│  apache{cynthiah}1: telnet lingua.utdallas.edu 8888                    ▼ │
│ ◀ ▥                                                                  ▶   │
└──────────────────────────────────────────────────────────────────────────┘
```

FIGURE 2.8   UNIX Telnet Connect Script

FIGURE 2.9   Pueblo World List Setup

20

Because most client programs vary in the way they require you to enter this information, we must refer you to the manual or help system for the particular program you are using for information on how to do this.

If you are having trouble connecting to a MOO using its domain name, try using its IP number instead, if you know it. It could well be that the MOO is functioning all right, but the server that looks up domain names is down or not responding.

e

Connecting with enCore Xpress

To connect to an enCore 2.0-based MOO using the enCore Xpress system, you must use a Web browser that has the features needed to run Xpress. At the time of this writing, on the Macintosh and Linux platforms this means Netscape Communicator 4.5 or newer, and on the Windows 95, 98, and NT platforms this means Netscape Communicator 4.5 or Microsoft Internet Explorer 4.0 or newer versions.

As in the case of connecting with a traditional MOO client, you must also specify both a domain name and a port number when using Xpress. In this case, however, this information should be given in the form of a URL:

http://someserver.somesite.edu:7000/

Most enCore Xpress systems are using port 7000, but variations may occur. Figure 2.10 shows an enCore Xpress login page.

!

The enCore Xpress system uses certain advanced features of your Web browser that you may not have given any thought to before. These are called Java, JavaScript, and Cookies. If you experience problems while using Xpress, the problem is most likely that one or more of these features are not turned on. To correct this problem, open your browser's preference settings and make sure they are all enabled.

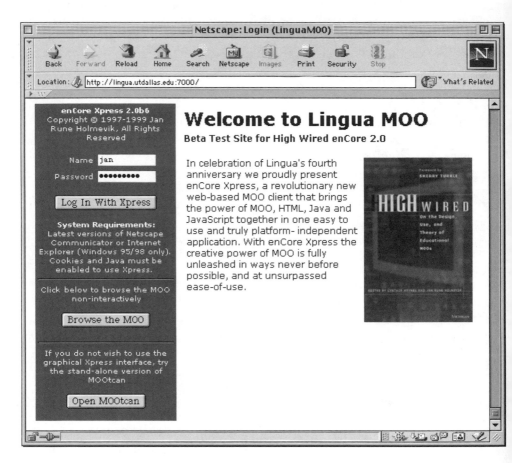

FIGURE 2.10   Example of enCore Xpress Login Page

Connecting Using the BioGate System

Connecting to a MOO that has the BioGate system installed is essentially the same as connecting with enCore Xpress. You must first point your Web browser to the login page (see Figure 2.11), and then type your login name and password to connect.

At the time of this writing, Web browsers known to work with the BioGate system are Netscape Navigator 3.0 and newer (Win95, Unix) and Microsoft Internet Explorer (Win95). For more information on the BioGate system we invite you to take a look at BioMOO at http://bioinformatics. weizmann.ac.il:8888/ or Diversity University, Inc. at http://moo.du.org:8000/

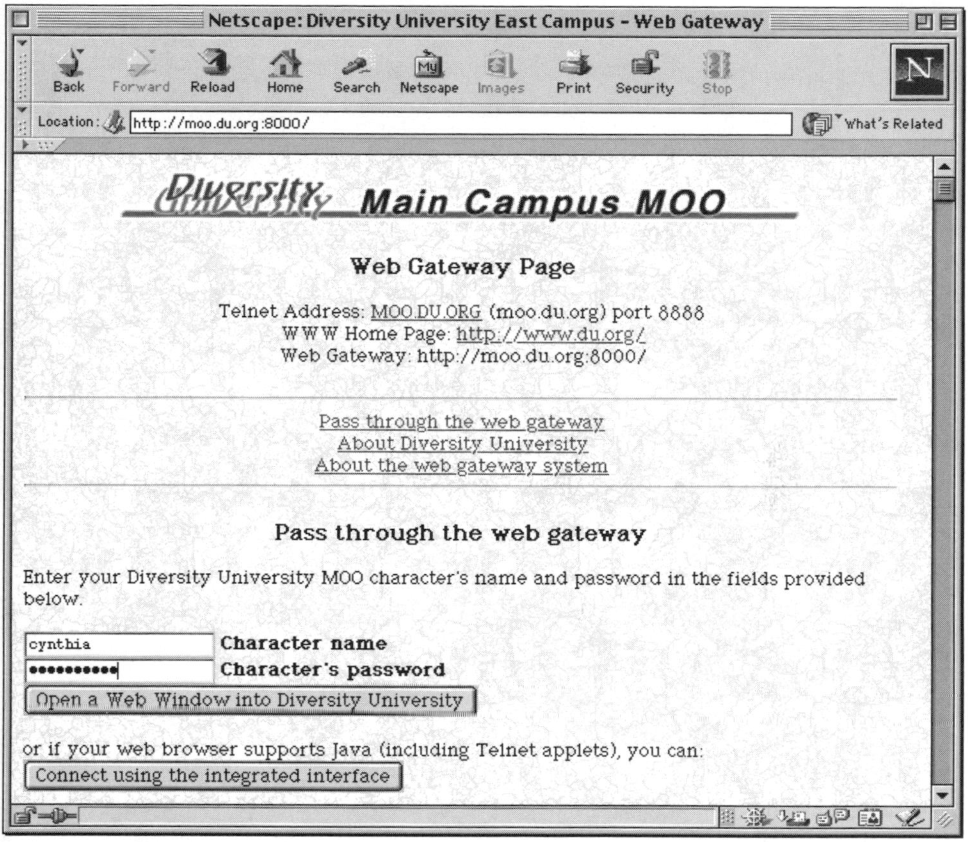

```
┌─────────────────────────────────────────────────────────────────────────┐
│ □ ═══════ Netscape: Diversity University East Campus - Web Gateway ═══ 冃冃 │
│  ┌───┐ ┌───┐ ┌───┐ ┌───┐ ┌───┐ ┌───┐ ┌───┐ ┌───┐ ┌───┐ ┌───┐      ┌───┐  │
│  │ ◀ │ │ ▶ │ │ ↻ │ │ ⌂ │ │ 🔍│ │My │ │ 🖼│ │ 🖨│ │ 🔒│ │ ⊗ │      │ N │  │
│  Back  Forward Reload  Home  Search Netscape Images  Print Security Stop  └───┘  │
│  Location: 🔖 http://moo.du.org:8000/                          🗐 What's Related │
```

Diversity University *Main Campus MOO*

Web Gateway Page

Telnet Address: MOO.DU.ORG (moo.du.org) port 8888
WWW Home Page: http://www.du.org/
Web Gateway: http://moo.du.org:8000/

———

Pass through the web gateway
About Diversity University
About the web gateway system

———

Pass through the web gateway

Enter your Diversity University MOO character's name and password in the fields provided
below.

| cynthia | **Character name**

| •••••••••• | **Character's password**

[Open a Web Window into Diversity University]

or if your web browser supports Java (including Telnet applets), you can:

[Connect using the integrated interface]

FIGURE 2.11   Example of the BioGate System's Login Page

Welcome to the MOO

The first thing you will typically see on connecting to a MOO is the welcome
screen. This is the MOO's front door to the world. The welcome screen from
Lingua MOO in Figure 2.12 is an example of what you may see when you
first reach a MOO. Each MOO will feature its own special welcome screen,
but usually the welcome screen displays instructions on how to enter the
MOO, as well as information about its purpose and other important information related to the particular MOO.

To get inside the MOO, you can enter either as a guest or as a registered
user. The main difference between guests and registered users in a MOO has
to do with the number of privileges they have and the repertoire of commands

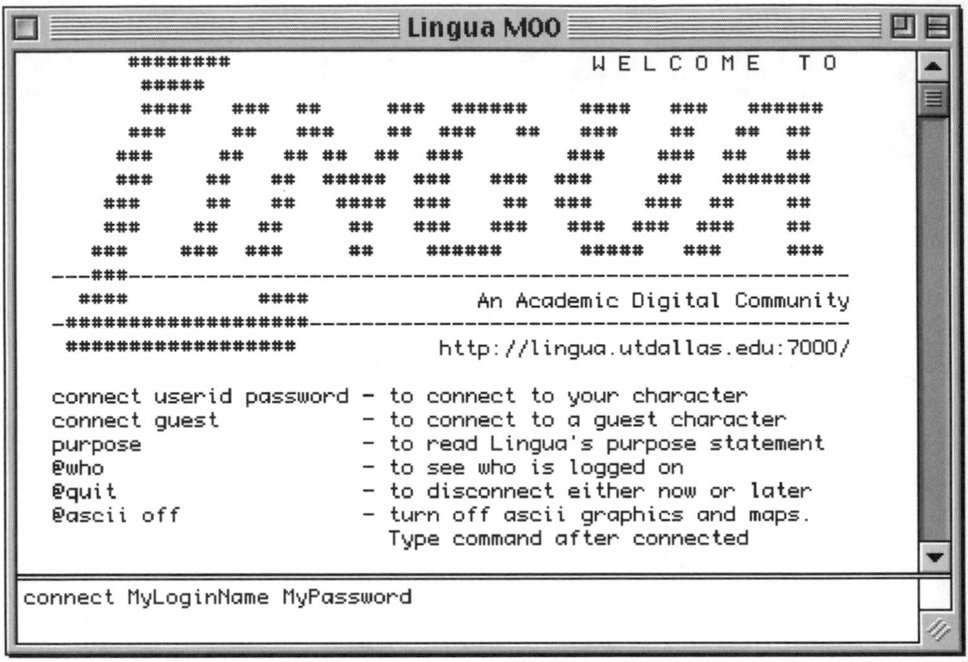

```
 ▣ ═══════════════════════ Lingua MOO ═══════════════════════ ▣ ▤
   ########                              W E L C O M E   T O      ▲
     #####                                                        ▓
     ####    ###  ##      ###  ######     ####    ###    ######
     ###     ##   ###     ##   ###   ##   ###     ##    ##   ##
     ###      ##   ## ##  ##   ###         ###    ###    ##   ##
     ###      ##   ##  ##### ###   ###    ###      ##   #######
     ###      ##   ##   ####  ###    ##   ###    ###    ##   ##
     ###     ##  ##     ##   ###   ###   ###   ###  ###     ##
     ###    ###  ###    ##   ######     #####  ###       ###
   ---###-------------------------------------------------------
     ####             ####          An Academic Digital Community
   -#################-------------------------------------------
     #################          http://lingua.utdallas.edu:7000/

   connect userid password - to connect to your character
   connect guest           - to connect to a guest character
   purpose                 - to read Lingua's purpose statement
   @who                    - to see who is logged on
   @quit                   - to disconnect either now or later
   @ascii off              - turn off ascii graphics and maps.
                             Type command after connected
                                                                 ▼
  ┌─────────────────────────────────────────────────────────────┐
  │ connect MyLoginName MyPassword                               │
  └─────────────────────────────────────────────────────────────┘
```

FIGURE 2.12   Example of Welcome Screen from Lingua MOO

or verbs (as they are called in the MOO) that they can use. Both guests and registered users can talk to others and explore the MOOscape; registered users may have the privilege to build new rooms and other objects, and maybe even program. Whether you use a MOO primarily as a guest or as a registered user will depend on your reasons for going to a particular MOO. In some cases, you may go to take part in class discussions, and in this case a guest account will let you do what you need to do. In other cases, you may be required to build a MOO room or write a MOO *cyphertext,* or perhaps program a conversational robot. In this case you will need a registered account at the MOO. We will return in detail to building and programming issues in following chapters, but first let us get you connected and teach you some of the basic communication and navigation skills you will need.

(i)

The word *cyphertext* combines *cyber, hyper,* and *text.* It combines in one word traditional one-dimensional, sequential text with two-dimensional hypertext. The third dimension is the presence of the reader/writer in the text itself. In a MOO we are what we write; our textual representations are what people see when they read us. Thus, the word *cyphertext* was coined to describe what a MOO is in textual terms.

Once you have reached the MOO's welcome screen you can connect as a guest by typing:

```
connect guest
```

Note that, as a guest, you are not required to give any password when you log in. Although some MOOs allow you to choose your own name when you log on as a guest, most MOOs will simply assign you a predefined guest name. In ATHEMOO, for example, which is an educational MOO in Hawaii dedicated to theater education, all guest accounts are named after famous people from the world of theater and literature such as Shakespeare, Dante, Ibsen, and so forth. Telnet to moo.hawaii.edu 9999 and type *connect guest*. If you are lucky, you will now be Shakespeare's Guest. If that particular guest account is in use, you will be some other famous literary figure's guest.

If you already have a character account in the MOO you are connecting to, you should enter your login name and password at this point.

```
connect login-name password
```

We talk more about how to get a registered character in Chapter 4. For now we'll assume that you connect and use the MOO as a guest.

N O T E S

1. Our chapter title is an obvious allusion to an early article on MOOs and writing classes written in May 1994 by David S. Bennahum for the magazine *Lingua Franca*. David's Web site contains some valuable links and is full of his various exploits in cyberspace. Check it out on the WWW at:

   http://memex.org/david.html

2. For a list of other MUD and MOO clients, please see

   http://web.nwe.ufl.edu/~tari/connections/client-info.html

EXERCISES

1. Find out what kind of client program your class is using when you meet on the MOO. Once you are logged on to the MOO, take notes on how the client works. View its various menu choices, preference settings, and session options. Experiment with the settings to see how they alter the MOO session window and input/output of text. Make notes in your MOO notebook. If you are in a lab or computer classroom, you should not alter the settings because the teacher or lab manager will have set those for all users. But if you have access to the Internet from home, go to the various Web sites already discussed and download various freeware MOO clients. Pick the one that suits your preferences and computer operating system (i.e., either Mac or PC).

2. Now it's time to log on to the MOO on your own, using the MOO client of your choice (or what is available in your classroom or lab). Using Appendix C, check out the various educational MOOs listed by actually logging on as a guest. Keep notes in your MOO notebook about guest restrictions and features available to guests. Note any welcome screen information that pertains to guest players, such as where to obtain help texts for the MOO, where to explore, who to contact for questions, and so forth. Use your notebook to compare procedures and accessibility to online help guides on various MOOs. During the next class time, share your findings with the class. (Your teacher may assign groups of students to explore the MOOs listed in Appendix C, in which case your reports to the class will make the process more efficient and faster.)

3 The Newbie School: Learning the Bare Basics

Help, I'm Lost!

One of the most common reactions among people who enter a MOO for the first time is: "Help, I'm lost!" The sense of dislocation, the uneasy feeling of disembodiment, and a general lack of overview that often accompanies the first few MOO visits are things that every newbie experiences. But we can assure you that once you get more experience with the MOO environment, you will start to feel much more comfortable and at home.

(i)

New MOOers are often called *newbies*. Veteran MOOers, or people who have used MOOs for a while but still remember what it's like to be a newbie, will often go out of their way to help new users. So don't be afraid to ask for help. Getting to know other people from other parts of the world is one of the most rewarding and fun aspects of the MOO experience.

Despair Not, Help Is Nearby

Before you learn how to use the MOO and its many commands, what will probably seem the most daunting is gaining an overview of what the commands are and how to use them. In this book we can cover only the most frequently used commands, and the things we talk about will probably not answer all your immediate questions. It is, therefore, important that you learn how to use and take advantage of the MOO's online help system. This help system is quite comprehensive and will, in most cases, provide you with the answers you seek. Learning how to use it early on will save you a lot of trouble and frustration later. Type *help* to start exploring the help system.

(i)

In a MOO there are basically two types of commands, or verbs as they are called: (1) the VR-commands (virtual reality commands) you use to interact with objects in the virtual world, and (2) the system commands that you use to control the MOO system itself. The @ symbol is used to denote system commands that belong to the second category. For example, when you type *@quit* to leave the MOO, this is a command that you give to the MOO system, as opposed to *look,* which is a command that you use to interact with the virtual reality of the MOO.

For your reference, in Appendix A we have included a list of common verbs found in most MOOs. Most of these verbs are well documented, and in the MOO you can type *help verb-name* at any time to find out what a particular verb does and how to use it. For example, if you wish to find out more about how to use the *@examine* verb that we will talk about in a bit, you type *help @examine.*

You can also get help on how to use many of the objects that you find around the MOO by typing *help object-name.* If the particular object you are looking at is annotated with a help text, it will be displayed on your screen. To find out more about how to use a MOO recorder you come across called Jan's Recorder, you type *help Jan's Recorder.*

The enCore Xpress Graphical
MOO Interface

(e)

The enCore Xpress system's visual point-and-click interface is probably easier and more intuitive to understand for new MOOers than is the traditional text-based interface and command-line system. In its standard configuration this interface consists of three separate areas on the main Xpress user screen, as shown in Figure 3.1.

On top you'll find the Xpress toolbar, which provides easy access to all the powerful and creative features of MOO such as mailing, object creation, editing, programming, and more. The toolbar on your screen may not have as many buttons as shown in Figure 3.1 because the number of toolbar options will depend on the kind of *player class* your MOO character belongs to. (See Chapter 4 for more on player classes in MOO.) To the left is the talk, or chat area, which is where you communicate with other MOO users by typing

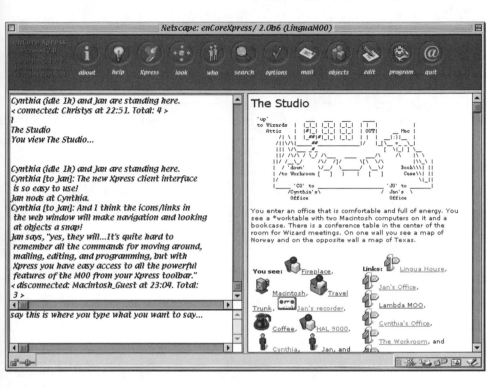

FIGURE 3.1   enCore Xpress Main User Screen

what you want to say. The right area of the screen is called the Web window, and here you will see descriptions of rooms and objects you explore, as well as links you can follow for further exploration.

Exploring the MOOscape

After you have entered the MOO, either as a guest or as a registered user, you will typically land in a central location such as the Courtyard of Lingua MOO (Figure 3.2) or the Lobby in ATHEMOO (Figure 3.3). In a well-designed educational MOO, this central location should give you easy access to most of the MOO's main areas such as classrooms, player quarters, and the various resources that the MOO hosts. In large MOOs, such as Diversity University, you may have the option of starting in a quiet place where you can review help texts and other online reference materials before you venture out into the more "noisy" MOOscape.

One of the most frequently used verbs in the MOO is *look*. This is the verb that will let you explore your surroundings as you venture around in

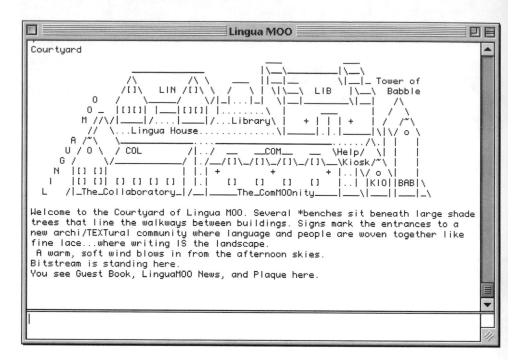

FIGURE 3.2   The Courtyard of Lingua MOO

```
Lobby

Welcome to the ATHEMOO lobby! The lobby is brightly lit and looks
like a fun, comfortable place to be.    From here you can see that
in the Dancer's Barre and Grille there is a festively decorated
cart with champagne to celebrate ATHEMOO's Second Birthday.
Go in and try some - it's on the house!

Beginners, to speak to others, type say and hit enter.  The computer
will prompt you for your message after which you hit enter again.

Why not try ATHEMOO's new tutorial?  Type @tutorial and hit enter.


You see Lobby Clock, Credits, ATHEMOO News, Sign to Kafka Project, and Welcome
to ATHEMOO! here.
Obvious exits: east to Stairwell, north to Courtyard, bar to Dancer's Barre and
Grill, desk to Registration Desk, ZeNews to Newsstand, up to Whine and Cheese
Balcony, and west to GNA Forum (ATHEMOO)
```

FIGURE 3.3   The Lobby in ATHEMOO

the MOOscape. You can use the *look* verb to take a closer look at anything you see, including rooms you visit, objects you find, and other users that you encounter. To see how the room you're in looks, just type *look*. To get information about the objects around you, including yourself and other users, you type:

```
look object
Example: look news - to see the description of the news
paper
```

What the *look* verb shows you is a textual description of the object you are looking at. For example, if we look at an old battered travel trunk we have in our Studio at Lingua MOO we see the following description:

```
look Travel Trunk

Travel Trunk
You see a large turn-of-the-century travel trunk with travel
stickers all over it from Cairo, Athens, Paris, Oslo,
Dallas, Singapore, Taos, and all kinds of exotic places.
```

(i)

For convenience, the *look* verb can be shortened to just *l*. You can look at yourself by typing *look me*, and you can look at the room you are in by typing *look here* or just *look*. After you enter a room where people are talking, the description of the room will eventually scroll off the top of your screen as the text of the conversation continues. To make the room description reappear on your screen, just type *look* (or click on the LOOK button on the Xpress toolbar).

Most objects that you encounter in your MOO wanderings are interactive in one way or another. That is, you can do things with them besides just looking at them. For example, you can read a sign you come across, open a trunk, and drink a bottle of virtual juice. In most cases you will be able to deduce what you can do with an object, either based on its functionality or hints in its description. Other times, however, it may be harder to guess what you can do with an object, and in this case you can use the *@examine* verb to see additional verbs you can use to manipulate the object. In the example below we use *@examine* to find additional ways to interact with a pot of hot coffee found in our Studio.

```
@examine coffee
Coffee (#444) is owned by Bitstream (#100).
```

```
Aliases: Coffee
You see a pot of hot freshly brewed coffee! Why not 'drink
coffee'?
Key: (None.)
Obvious Verbs:
  drink coffee
  g*et/t*ake coffee
  d*rop/th*row coffee
  gi*ve/ha*nd coffee to <anything>
  v*iew coffee
  dis*play coffee
  connect coffee to <anything>
```

Most objects that you find can be picked up and carried around. In a room you may find a note that you would like to read. To pick it up simply type *take note*. You will now be holding on to the note until you put it down by typing *drop note*.

(!)

Please remember to leave things where you found them (i.e., *drop* the object after you have taken it). In many cases, the owner of an object has left it there so that visitors may enjoy it, and if you walk away with the object, it may take a while before the owner realizes it's gone and can move it back. To find out what you are holding or carrying around with you, you can type *inventory* or simply *i* at any time. It is quite common for new MOOers to forget to leave things they have picked up, so please keep this in mind as you explore the MOO.

Getting Around

One of the fun things to do in a MOO is to venture around and explore rooms and objects that other users have designed and written. Now that you know how to look at things and examine them more closely, we are ready to show you how to get around and explore.

There are basically two ways you can move around in the MOO. The first is by moving from room to room using exits, and the other is by *teleporting* from one location to another. Exits are doorways or *cypherlinks* to other locations in the MOO, and in every room that has exits, they are listed either at the bottom of your screen, or if there is a map, perhaps marked by a letter code on the map itself. (The Xpress client graphic window will list the exits as links you simply select in order to go there.) To move in a given direction simply type the name of the direction or exit. For example, if you see an exit named *west*, you type *west* to go there, or if a code on the map says "LIB," you type *LIB* to use that exit. If you get lost, which can frequently happen in MOOs that you don't know or are unfamiliar with, you can always get back to where you started by typing *home*. Unless you have a room of your own in the MOO and have designated it to be your home (more on this later), typing *home* anywhere in the MOO will transport you directly back to the starting point where you first logged in.

A fast and convenient way to move around the MOO is by teleporting directly to a location. If you think teleporting sounds a bit futuristic, keep in mind that in the textual reality of MOO anything is possible. Illusions are created through means of text in the same way you find in a novel, a short story, or a poem. The difference is that in the MOO you are part of the story—part of an unfolding textual experience. The teleport verbs that you will find in most MOOs are *@join* and *@go*. Other variations of these verbs may exist, and some MOOs may not have them at all.

The *@go* verb will let you teleport directly to a room that you specify. For example, in Lingua MOO, typing *@go Courtyard* will teleport you directly to the Courtyard from anywhere in the MOO. Sometimes there may be more than one room with the same name, in which case *@go* will not be able to determine which room you wish to go to. If this happens, you can use the room's *object number* to specify where you want to go.

Every object in the MOO has its own unique object number that consists of a pound sign (#) followed by the object's number. For example, the object number of MOO-object number 100 has the following format: #100. If you know the object number of an object, you can use it instead of its name when you refer to the object. Let's say that *Jan's Recorder* used in the example above has object number #100. You can look at it by either typing *look Jan's Recorder* or *look #100*. Also note that since the object number is unique to an object, you can use it to refer to objects anywhere in the MOO. Similarly, you can only refer to an object by name if it happens to be in the same room as you are, or if you are holding it.

Ⓔ

If you are using enCore Xpress, you can easily explore the MOOscape simply by clicking on the links for objects and exits that you'll see on your screen (see Figure 3.4).

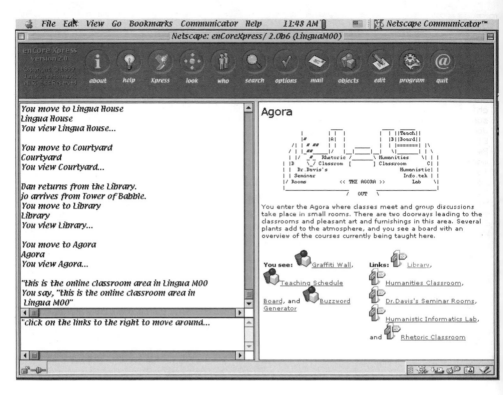

FIGURE 3.4   Exploring the MOOscape with Xpress

Who Is Online?

Before we introduce you to the @*join* verb, let us first mention another useful verb that you will be using a lot, namely, @*who*. Typing this command at any time will display a list of all the people who are connected to the MOO at the time you type the command, as illustrated in Figure 3.5.

In addition to telling you the user names of people who are currently online, the @*who* listing will show you how long they have been connected to the MOO, how long since they last typed something, and where in the MOO they are.

Depending on the configuration of the MOO, real names and e-mail addresses of users may also be available, and, if this is the case, another useful command that you can use in all enCore-based educational MOOs is @*whois*.

```
┌──────────────────────────────────────────────────────────────────────┐
│ □  ▓▓▓▓▓▓▓▓▓▓▓▓▓▓▓▓▓▓▓▓▓▓  Lingua MOO ▓▓▓▓▓▓▓▓▓▓▓▓▓▓▓▓▓▓▓▓▓▓   ▣ ▤ │
├──────────────────────────────────────────────────────────────────────┤
│ Name                      Connected     Idle time   Location        ▲ │
│ ────                      ─────────     ─────────   ────────          │
│ Jan (#2)                  9 seconds     0 seconds   The Studio         │
│ MagdalinPeter (#136)      18 minutes    a second    Humanities Classroom│
│ CameronHonsa (#222)       16 minutes    2 seconds   Foucault           │
│ PaulSulwer (#4566)        14 minutes    6 seconds   Foucault           │
│ AdrianDelgado (#4552)     15 minutes    6 seconds   Foucault           │
│ chintan (#229)            13 minutes    7 seconds   Joyce              │
│ sun (#237)                10 minutes    8 seconds   Humanities Classroom│
│ JohnF. (#4549)            19 minutes    8 seconds   Eco                │
│ ElizabethReyes (#233)     18 minutes    10 seconds  Joyce              │
│ BelleSarkar (#224)        12 minutes    13 seconds  Heidegger          │
│ mariapacheco (#564)       12 minutes    14 seconds  Humanities Classroom│
│ tonyantonelli (#4550)     19 minutes    14 seconds  Heidegger          │
│ ron (#226)                20 minutes    21 seconds  Heidegger          │
│ Sarah (#2168)             22 minutes    37 seconds  Humanities Classroom│
│ JillDelaTorre (#562)      15 minutes    47 seconds  Joyce              │
│ andrelulla (#4555)        19 minutes    53 seconds  Humanities Classroom│
│ ElinaMargolina (#1718)    17 minutes    58 seconds  Foucault           │
│ MichaelG. (#4548)         19 minutes    a minute    Humanities Classroom│
│ Tong (#99)                22 minutes    a minute    Eco                │
│ annastypula (#4562)       11 minutes    2 minutes   Eco                │
│ ChariceDelRosario (#4564) 19 minutes    2 minutes   Eco                │
│ HildeC (#3877)            5 minutes     2 minutes   Cornys Corner      │
│ Cynthia (#84)             an hour       2 minutes   The Studio         │
│ Klaus (#3917)             an hour       4 minutes   Waldcafe "Zum Hirschen"│
│ Deya (#1720)              17 minutes    8 minutes   Humanities Classroom│
│ Britt (#4039)             2 hours       37 minutes  Britt's Lodge    ▓ │
│                                                                        │
│ Total: 26 players, 24 of whom have been active recently.            ▼ │
├──────────────────────────────────────────────────────────────────────┤
│ │                                                                      │
└──────────────────────────────────────────────────────────────────────┘
```

FIGURE 3.5   *@who* Listing from Lingua MOO, March 4, 1998

This command will display a list of connected users similar to the *@who* listing, except that it will list people's real names and e-mail addresses. This is particularly useful if you want to contact someone for further work and collaboration, or if you need to look up someone's e-mail address. If you use a player's name after the *@whois* command, for example *@whois Cynthia,* it will also provide more detailed information about that person, for example, their home page URL, research interests, and more. We will return to how you can also set up this information for yourself a bit later in the chapter.

The *@join* command that we mentioned previously, as the name implies, is used to join someone by teleporting to the room or location he or she is in. If, for example, the *@who* listing tells you that there is another user online named Cynthia, you can join her by typing *@join Cynthia.* There are, however, certain commonsense rules you need to apply when you want to join another player. We remember some of our own first embarrassing moments when we barged in on a MOO administrator's meeting at MediaMOO without knocking first! Needless to say, it was awkward. One of the administrators was kind enough to page us privately and ask us to move into the next MOO room, whereupon she explained that we had come in to a staff meeting unannounced. That's learning the hard way! So save yourself some embarrassment and always ask first!

People come to the MOO for many different reasons, some to work, others to hang out or visit with friends. Out of courtesy, you should always ask before you join someone. For example, if you want to talk to Cynthia, you should type @*knock Cynthia* first to see if she's free to talk. If she is not busy and wants to talk to you, she can reply with @*invite player-name* (for example, @*invite Jan*). Sometimes you may be too busy to talk, and in this case you can reply with @*busy player-name.* This tells the person who knocked on your door that you are busy at the moment, but that they should try contacting you again later. The @*knock,* @*invite,* and @*busy* commands are available in all enCore-based MOOs and many others as well.

Communicating with Other People

Talking and Paging

One thing that people probably enjoy most about MOOs is talking to others and getting to know people from other parts of the country and even the world. In what follows, we discuss two ways that communication happens in the MOO environment. The first, and by far the most common, is by *talking,* that is, by writing what you want to say. The second is to express yourself through use of textual body language, also called *emoting.* We'll begin by showing you how you talk to other people in the MOO. To talk to someone in the same room as you are, you type *say* followed by what you want to say, like this:

```
say Hello there!
You see: You say, "Hello there!"
Everyone else in the room sees: Jan says "Hello there!"
```

Note that one double quotation mark can conveniently be used instead of the *say* verb as demonstrated below.

```
"hi, how are you?
You see: You say, "Hi, how are you?"
Everyone else in the room sees: Jan says "Hi, how are you?"
```

Many people find it hard and somewhat awkward to write instead of speaking in a MOO. For one thing, typing something takes longer than speaking it, and therefore slow typists tend to take a long time to express themselves in the MOO. But keep in mind that writing is the major goal in a writing course! After all, writing in virtual real-time situations is a wonderful way to increase your dexterity in typing, your thinking fast on your feet (so to speak), and your ability to use your imagination to write in narrative and descriptive styles. When you describe your player persona and your room and objects, your writing must convey your creativity. In addition, you will find that you use more active verbs, more variation in word choice, as you learn how to communicate to other MOO players. Writing in the MOO also enables you to practice English as a second language, if English is not your native language (for information about other language learning and ESL MOOs, see Chapter 9).

With all this writing, your speed and ability to adapt will come in time, though you may experience frustration at first. The fluidity of a typical MOO discussion, where many different threads of discussion may be going on at once, is very different and unfamiliar from the visual face-to-face discourse that we are normally used to. Combined, these things usually prove to be the hardest challenges to master for new MOO users. One way that you can make it easier to express yourself, therefore, is to speak in shorter segments, that is, to divide what you want to say into two or more shorter phrases or sentences.

```
Jan says, "Here is an example of how you can split up a
longer statement into shorter segments..."
Jan says, "so that it's easier to type. End a line with
three dots..."
Jan says, "to signal that you are not through talking."
```

By segmenting your talk in this manner you avoid the frustration of finding that others have moved on to a new topic by the time you are through crafting a long and intricate sentence.

Often, when several people are in the same room, you may want to address a particular person. To do that, type *to* followed by the name of the person you want to talk to, and then what you want to say.

```
to Cynthia Good to see you again:-).
You, Cynthia, and everyone else in the room sees:
Jan [to Cynthia]: Good to see you again:-)
```

Please note that there must be a space between the *to* command and the name of the person you wish to address.

You can also communicate with people who are online elsewhere in the MOO by using the *page* command. *Page* sends a private message to the person you indicate, and can thus also be used as a whisper command. In the example below, Jan sends a private page to Cynthia who is in a different room in the MOO. On her screen Cynthia sees:

```
You sense that Jan is looking for you in The Studio.
He pages, "Hi, may I join you?"
```

In enCore-based MOOs, a hyphen (-) can be used in place of the word *page*. Please note that there should be no space between the hyphen and the name of the person you wish to page.

```
-Cynthia Hi, do you have a minute for a question?
```

You can also reply to the last person who paged you by simply typing a hyphen followed by what you want to say. Note that there must be a space between the hyphen and your phrase. So, for example, if Cynthia wants to reply to the page from Jan, she can type:

```
- yes, sure, come on over.
```

Keep in mind that the *page* reply function will always send your message to the last person who paged you. So, if you have several players paging you, you may need to use the *page* command instead of the shortcut to make sure you send the right message to the right player.

If you page or talk to someone, and they do not respond to you right away, check the @*who* listing to see if they are still connected and how long they have been *idle*. If it shows that the person you want to talk to has not been active recently, it may mean that they are not sitting at their computer at the moment, or that they may be working on something else in a different window. It could also mean that they have lost their connection to the MOO. It is always frustrating when you try to talk to somebody without getting any response, so please remember that there are many reasons why someone may not respond to a page right away.

Emote and Remote–Emote

Using body language, also called *emoting,* is another common way to express yourself in the MOO environment. Although this may sound a little strange given the textual nature of the MOO, it is in fact one of the most powerful and flexible ways you can communicate with other people online. Emoting is usually achieved by typing a *colon* (:) followed by your *emote.* For example, if you want to express a smile you type:

```
:smiles
You and everyone else in the room sees: Jan smiles.
```

If you want to stand on your head and wiggle your toes in the air while saying something, you can easily do that by typing

```
:stands on his head wiggling his toes in the air and says,
This is pretty cool:)
You and everyone else in the room sees: Jan stands on his
head wiggling his toes in the air and says, This is pretty
cool:).
```

As you will see from these two examples, the *emote* command is very flexible and can be used to express just about anything you wish. For example, after entering a room full of people you may wish to type:

```
:smiles and waves to everyone.
You and everyone else in the room sees: Jan smiles and waves
to everyone.
```

Because the whole MOO experience is so textually infused, you can achieve a lot by being creative in your use of emotes.

Just as you can talk to someone at a distance using the *page* command, you can also *emote* things to a person in a different room. This is called *remote-emoting,* and, just like a page, it sends a private message to a person that you specify. A remote–emote is achieved by typing a plus symbol (+) followed by the name of the person you wish to contact and finally the text you wish to emote.

```
+Cynthia waves
Cynthia sees: (From the Studio) Jan waves.
```

Again, as with *page,* you can reply to the last person who contacted you either with a page or a remote-emote simply by typing a plus symbol followed by your emote. For example, Cynthia can easily reply to Jan by typing:

```
+ waves back and says, Good morning!
Jan sees: (From Cynthia's Office) Cynthia waves back and
says, Good morning!
```

Managing and Troubleshooting the Interface

Output Control and Delimiter

If you are using Telnet as your MOO client program, the text you type in may get disrupted and broken up by the output from the MOO. This can be very confusing and frustrating, and the best way to deal with it is to get a good MOO client program. If, for various reasons, you cannot use a MOO client, you can still use the built-in output control system to prevent your input from being broken up by the output from the MOO. Just type one double quotation mark (") and hit the return key. You can now type your input without interruptions, and the output from the MOO will be suspended until you hit return again. In addition you can use an *output delimiter* to separate your output from everyone else's. Type *@delimiter on* to activate the output delimiter system. Typing *@delimiter off* deactivates it.

Page Buffering

If you don't have a client program that allows you to scroll back, and you are having trouble with text scrolling off your screen, you should try the command *@pagelength 24.* This will instruct the MOO to display only twenty-four lines at a time. If the text you are reading is longer than this, you will be prompted to type *@more* when ready to read the next twenty-four lines, and so forth. Type *@pagelength 0* to turn page buffering off.

Line Length

With some clients programs, you may only be able to read the beginning of lines. The problem in this case is that your client program does not wrap long lines. To solve this problem, you can either check the preferences for your client program to see if you can set it to do so, or you can have the MOO wrap long lines for you. Type *@wrap on* to instruct the MOO to wrap long lines; *@wrap off* turns line-wrapping off.

Local Echo

If, after connecting to the MOO, you cannot see what you type, you may need to look at the preferences in your Telnet or MOO client program to make sure that the option *local echo* is turned on. If you cannot find such an option in the client program you are using, please consult the manual or online help system for that particular program. There is, unfortunately, no way the MOO can help you with this because it is a client-related problem.

MOO Netiquette and Manners

As you have probably discovered by now, the MOO environment is a place that encourages learning in fun and playful ways. However, you should note that there are several norms for appropriate behavior that must be followed in order for everyone to enjoy their MOO experience. Most MOOs have their own policies with regard to this, so always be sure to type *help manners* whenever you log on to a new MOO. Generally speaking, however, let us just point out a few things that you should keep in mind when you are in a MOO.

- Don't do things online that you wouldn't normally do in other situations. This includes offensive language or actions.
- Be nice and friendly, and don't bother or harass other users.
- Don't spy on other people and never log private conversations with the intent of publishing them.
- Don't walk off with other people's objects unless they have given you permission to do so.
- Be cautious when using humor, irony, or sarcasm. Remember that people in the MOO may come from diverse cultural backgrounds and what may be funny to you could be offensive to them.
- Don't join other people unless you have knocked first and received an invitation. Remember that people come to the MOO for many different reasons, and just because they are online does not mean they are free to talk to you.

MOOs are generally not strict environments where social conduct is closely monitored. As we mentioned in Chapter 1, you should, however, be aware that failure to adhere to rules outlined above could cause you to lose your account in the MOO. Furthermore, depending on the actions taken by the MOO's administrators and your teacher, it could also have wider implications for the class you are taking and even affect future studies at your university. Just because you are sitting behind a computer isolated from the people you are talking to does not mean that you are in any way anonymous. On the contrary, the MOO administrators usually have access to much information about you and your whereabouts, which can easily be used to locate you and hold you responsible for your actions. There are several examples of sexual harassment cases online that have caused people to be expelled from school or lose their jobs. So be responsible and help make the MOO a fun and productive learning experience for everyone.

In this chapter you have learned the basic skills that you need in order to use a MOO. In the following chapters we will talk about how you can broaden these skills to include things such as getting a permanent account, building a virtual room for yourself, and even how to program simple MOO objects yourself. Before you log out by typing *@quit*, however, please bear in mind that one of the most useful commands for new MOO users is this one:

```
say Hi, I'm new here. Do you have a minute for a question?
```

CLASS DISCUSSION

1. Discuss the dynamics of MOO talk and emotes in terms of how "text" affects you in a conversation in which you are not F2F. Give specific examples (which you have noted in your MOO notebook) of situations in which what you say and emote has introduced you to a new effect. Hold this discussion on the MOO. Now get into different groups in your RL classroom and discuss what happened online and how it affected you.

2. Discuss how interactive online behavior based on textual descriptions differs from RL interaction. List as many ways as you can, as a class, the differences you notice. Try to step outside of your traditional way of thinking about interaction among you and your teacher and classmates. What possibilities are opened up for changing how you interact? Are there factors that inhibit or encourage different modes of interaction? What is your first impression based on your interactive experiences?

EXERCISES

1. Log on to the MOOs of your choice (or the MOO your teacher is using). Then make notes about the various MOO welcome screens and welcome areas where you first connect. How are the designs helpful or not to a new MOOer? What are the MOO's theme and purpose?

2. Look at the various *help manners* texts at the MOOs you visit. Identify problem areas of behavior and make notes about how to avoid harassment from others online. Keep notes on situations you may encounter in which you felt uncomfortable, and discuss these with your teacher. Try to specify why you felt uncomfortable and whether you could have contributed to the situation or not.

3. Visit at least ten of the MOO's public spaces (you'll need to explore on your own), making notes about how exits were listed, where they led, and how you got back to your beginning location. Pay attention to the messages you saw on your screen as you entered and exited various rooms, and make notes about ones you like. You may want to customize your entrance and exit messages to your own MOO room at a later time.

4. Examine at least ten objects and make notes in your notebook about the obvious verbs associated with those objects. List the objects along with their object numbers and note any error messages you may see while examining the objects. Try to discover what you did wrong, or, if the object is not working, make a note of it and follow up by asking your teacher or the owner of the MOO object.

5. Practice talking, paging, and emoting on the MOO. Refer to the MOO manners by typing *help manners* and keeping notes about things to avoid or policies that may prove helpful in unexpected disagreeable situations. Try creating your own emotes in addition to using preprogrammed emotes that may be available on some MOOs. Write the custom emotes in your notebook so you can remember them. Be as creative as you can without being offensive.

4 Becoming a MOO Citizen

While using the MOO as a guest lets you walk around, explore, and talk to other people online, you can really only experience the full potential of the MOO as a registered user. By becoming a registered user in a MOO you receive your own personal *character* (sometimes called *player*) that you can use every time you are online. The registration process varies from MOO to MOO, as do the requirements for joining, but generally the procedure is as follows. Log on to the MOO as a guest and type:

```
@request character-name for email-address
```

For example, if you want to be known as Ann in the MOO, and your e-mail address is ann@someplace.edu, you would type:

```
@request Ann for ann@someplace.edu
```

(i)

In the MOO, users are often referred to as *characters* or *players.* These terms stem from the days when MOOs and MUDs were predominantly online role-playing games. As you become more familiar with the MOO, you will discover many other traces of MOOs' gaming origins. After the publication of Neal Stephenson's popular cyberspace novel, *Snow Crash,* in 1992, the word *avatar* has also come into use in reference to one's MOO persona.

Your character request is sent to the MOO's administrators who will process it and create the character for you. Please note that in large MOOs it may take up to several days before your request is processed. If your request is granted, the MOO administrators will send a character name, which is the same as your login name, and password to the e-mail address you provide, so be sure that your e-mail address is entered correctly. All user names in the MOO must be unique, and if someone is already using the name you want, you will be asked to pick a different name.

Many educational MOOs require that you give your full name and a statement as to why you wish to apply for a character. If the MOO has such a policy, you will be asked to enter this information as part of your character request. Please take your time when entering this information as the success of your application may depend on the validity of your reasons for wanting an account.

If your application is successful, you will receive your login name and password via e-mail. Passwords are usually generated using random letters, some of which may be upper case, and some, lower case. When you log on to the MOO as described in Chapter 2, you should note that passwords are *case sensitive,* meaning that there is a difference between caps and lower caps letters. For example, the passwords *bergen* and *Bergen* are not the same word. Failing to enter the password correctly is a common mistake that can easily be avoided by paying close attention when logging on and typing the password exactly as it appears in the e-mail that you get from the MOO.

Creating Your MOO Persona

The very first thing you should do after you connect to your new MOO character is to describe yourself, set your gender, and change your password to a word of your choice.

In enCore-based MOOs you can set all these preferences as well as many others simply by typing @*preferences* and following the directions on your screen, which at Lingua MOO range from 1 to 10 (Figure 4.1). enCore Xpress users can also set all these preferences easily by just clicking on the Options button in their Xpress toolbar (Figure 4.2).

If the MOO you are using is not based on the enCore MOO database, you may have to set each of these preferences individually. In the following section, we discuss each of the three most important preferences that everyone should set, and how to do so in non-enCore-based MOOs.

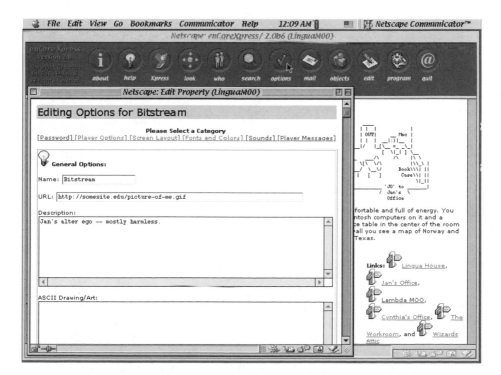

```
┌─────────────────────────────── Lingua MOO ═══════════════════════┬─┬─┐
│ □ ═══════════════════════════ Lingua MOO ═══════════════════════ ⊡ ⊟ │
│         UTTIUE                         UTTIUE                    ▲
│ You enter an office that is comfortable and full of energy. You see a *worktable
│ with two Macintosh computers on it and a bookcase. There is a conference table
│ in the center of the room for Wizard meetings. On one wall you see a map of
│ Norway and on the opposite wall a map of *Texas.
│
│ Cynthia (asleep) is standing here.
│ You see Fireplace, TV, Weather Map, MOO_evaluations, Macintosh, Honey & Cinnamon
│ Tea, Travel Trunk, Hologram, Planning-1/25, Music, Returned Mail, ATHEMOO
│ Hotline, Linguarians, VCR, Rubik's Cube, Jan's recorder, Generic Note Board, and
│ Champagne here.
│ @preferences
│ LINGUAMOO USER PREFERENCE SETUP
│ ================================
│ Please select one of the preferences below to change it.
│
│ Personal          Messages           Display
│ --------          --------           -------
│ 1) Name           7) Page Messages   9) Word Wrap
│ 2) Gender         8) Move Messages   10) Page Length
│ 3) Description
│ 4) Password
│ 5) Research
│ 6) Home Page
│
│ Please enter your choice (1-10), or type Q to quit          ▼
│ 3
└──────────────────────────────────────────────────────────────────┘
```

FIGURE 4.1   enCore Preference Setup

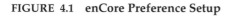

FIGURE 4.2   enCore Xpress User Preferences

(i)

The acronym RL, meaning "Real Life," is often used to distinguish between a person's MOO persona and their so-called real persona. Whereas this distinction was often useful back in the days when people used MOOs and MUDs mostly for role-playing games, it doesn't seem to work as well in educational MOOs where people are mostly identified by full names, and where the MOO persona is usually some variation of their "real" persona. As you will discover, there is nothing "virtual" about educational MOOs; they are real learning environments where real learning and serious activity take place.

Your Description

In the MOO you are what you write—you are the text other people read. For this reason you should invest some time in writing a good description for yourself. Whether you decide to write a description that closely matches your physical appearance, or whether you opt for something more creative is totally up to you. The way you use language to create images and illusions is really what MOOing is all about, so don't be afraid to let your creative juices flow. When you have decided on a description, you use the *@describe* verb:

```
@describe me as "Type your description here enclosed in
quote marks"
```

If you want a longer description that may span several lines of text, or if you want to edit your description later after you have entered it, we recommend that you use the MOO's text editor instead of the *@describe* verb. We will cover the MOO editors and how to use them in detail later.

Gender

Gender is one of the most important factors determining the way people relate to one another, and something that carries a lot of significance to all of us. In the MOO, you usually have several different gender options to choose from. The most common genders in MOO are neuter, male, female, either, Spivak, splat, plural, egotistical, royal, and 2nd. Please note that some MOOs may not support genders other than neuter, female, and male.

(i)

Computer *cross-dressing* is a term that has been coined to describe the kind of activity that often takes place in MUDs where females play male characters and vice versa. In socially oriented MOOs and MUDs, it is quite common for females to take on a male persona simply to avoid harassment from juvenile males, or for males to play female characters in order to get more attention. For this reason, on MOOs that have an anonymity policy, you can never really know whether the person you are talking to is male or female because their description and MOO gender are usually all you can know about them. In educational and other professional MOOs, computer cross-dressing is a less common practice due to their nonanonymity policies and more "serious" profiles.

Setting your gender is very simple. If you are in an enCore-based MOO, use the *@preferences* command. Otherwise, type *@gender* to see a list of available genders (like the ones listed above), choose the gender you want (for example, female), and type *@gender female*. This will set your gender to female, and will select female pronouns wherever appropriate when you speak and emote. You can change your gender at any time by repeating this procedure. On most MOOs you can also type *help gender* for additional instructions.

```
help gender
Showing help on '@gender':
----
Syntax: @gender <gender>
        @gender

The first form, with an argument, defines your player to have
the gender <gender>. If <gender> is one of the standard
genders (e.g., 'male', 'female', 'neuter',...), your various
pronouns will also be set appropriately, making exits and
certain other objects behave more pleasantly for you.

The second form tells you the current definition of your
player's gender, your current pronouns, and the complete
list of standard genders.

It should be noted that some of the "genders" on the
standard gender list need verb conjugation in order to work
properly and much of the MOO isn't set up for this (...yet).
For example, you should expect to see 'they is' a fair
amount if you @gender yourself 'plural'.
```

Changing Your Password

The password is your personal key to the MOO, and it is therefore of the utmost importance that you keep it secret at all times. If others should obtain your password, they can easily log in as you and do irreparable damage to your MOO creations, and, even worse, to your good name and reputation by impersonating you in the MOO. Therefore, be sure to change your password frequently by typing:

```
@password old-password new-password
```

There are a few general rules to remember when dealing with passwords.

- Change your password frequently, especially whenever you think it might have been compromised.
- Choose passwords that consist of at least six characters. The most secure passwords are those that are a combination of upper- and lowercase letters and numerals.
- Don't choose passwords that are easy to guess, like the name of your cat or your telephone number. On the other hand, don't choose passwords that are so hard to remember that you have to write them down.
- Never leave your password in places where others might find it, for example, on a piece of paper in the computer lab or classroom.
- Don't share your password with others; encourage them to apply for their own MOO character instead.

Your MOO password is encrypted using the same algorithm as the one that is being used in UNIX operating systems, so if you follow the general rules above, the chance that someone might actually break your secret password by chance is virtually negligible. In fact, your MOO password is so secure inside the MOO that not even the MOO administrators can read it. If you lose or forget it, they have to create a new password for you.

It is a common misconception that passwords are usually only stolen or broken by evil-minded *hackers* or *crackers* who use them to break in to computers on the Internet and steal or destroy classified information or other valuable data. Although this is a serious misconception of what computer hacking is really about, these are not the kind of people you normally have to worry about. After all, your MOO password is hardly the kind of password that will give access to highly classified military or other national security information, so it is not very likely that someone might actually spend a lot of time and effort trying to break it. Most passwords are in fact compromised not by being broken, but by being read in plain text. For this reason, be extra careful when you log on because the password you type will be readable to anyone who happens to see your screen. This is especially a problem in computer labs where people are sitting close together and it is easy to see what the person sitting next to you is doing.

Other Things You Can Customize

There are several other personal preferences in addition to the ones above that you may wish to set. The command @*messages me* will display some of them on your screen. The first part of the lines shown on your screen is actually a list of the commands you need to type in order to set that particular preference. For example, if you wish to set the message that others see when you enter a room, you should type @*oarrive me is "Jan arrives smiling and waving to everyone."* The last part of the command, which is enclosed in quotes, is the actual message that others see. For more information on messages, please type *help @messages.* Xpress users may simply select the Options button and scroll down until you see messages, then enter your text in those boxes, and click on Save.

Inhabitants of the MOO World

As we have discussed in previous chapters, in the MOO there are several different types of users. Just as there is a difference between guests and registered users, there are also differences between the various types of registered users. These differences have primarily to do with the kind of privileges each character type has.

Players

The basic character type in the MOO is called *player*. Like guests, any character of this type has the ability to walk around and talk to other people. In addition, players can set personal preferences like those we described above, send and receive mail in the MOO, participate in MOO newsgroups, and more. When you first become a registered user in a MOO, you usually start out as a player.

Builders

The next character type is called *builder.* Users that belong to this group can do everything that players can do; in addition, they have tools that allow them to add new rooms and other objects to the MOO. If, after having used the MOO for a while, you would like to become a builder in order to create your own room in the MOO, the administrators can easily *upgrade* your character to *builder.* In many educational MOOs, like Lingua MOO, for instance, everyone starts out as *builders.* In these MOOs we say that *builder* is the default *player class.*

Programmers

The third character type in the MOO is *programmer.* Programmers can do everything *players* and *builders* can, but they can also use the MOO's internal programming language to alter the functionality of the MOO itself in profound ways. If you would like to become a *programmer,* you should talk to the MOO administrators and kindly ask if you can have a *programmer bit.* The MOO programming language is quite powerful and relatively easy to learn. For those who are a little bit familiar with computer programming, we can say that MOO is an *object-oriented programming language* that resembles C or Java, but is syntactically easier and much less complex. More on this later.

Wizards

Wizards are the most powerful characters in the MOO. Actually, they are not wizards at all, but hardworking administrators and programmers who work behind the scenes to keep the MOO running smoothly. In this book, we use the words *wizards* and *administrators* interchangeably in reference to these MOO characters. Usually, because of all the responsibility, hard work, and time it takes to run a MOO, only a handful of people ever become *wizards.*

(i)

If you would like to try your hand at being a MOO *wizard,* it might be a good idea to start your own MOO. Our edited collection of essays, *High Wired: On the Design, Use and Theory of Educational MOOs,* published by University of Michigan Press, will teach you all you need to know to get your own MOO going.

We will deal with the *builder* and *programmer* character types in more detail in the chapters to follow, but first, let us talk some more about what you can do as a *player* character.

MOOmail

Composing and Sending MOOmail

Just as you can send e-mail to other people over the Internet, you can send *MOOmail* to other users in the MOO. MOOmail is internal to the MOO, but it functions like e-mail in that you are notified when you log in that you have mail messages waiting. In MOOs that support an anonymity policy, MOO-mail is, in fact, often the only way to communicate asynchronously with other MOO players. Sending a MOOmail involves using the MOO's built-in mail editor, which we will deal with in more detail in Chapter 5.

As with e-mail, sending a MOOmail involves:

- specifying one or more *recipients*
- entering a *subject* for your message
- typing the *MOOmail message* itself
- finally, *sending* it.

The command that is used to send MOOmail is called *@send*. Instead of using an e-mail address to specify a recipient, as you do with Internet mail, in the MOO you simply use the recipient's name as the address. For example, to send a MOOmail to someone named Diane, you simply type *@send Diane.* You can specify more than one recipient by adding more names, each separated by a space. To send the same message to both Diane and another person named Mark, you would type *@send Diane Mark.*

Whenever you invoke the MOOmail program, you are first asked to provide a word or phrase that aptly describes the subject of your message (see Figure 4.3). As with regular e-mail, try to come up with a word or phrase that describes the contents or purpose of your message as clearly as possible, so that the recipient can easily see what it is about.

A common mistake with MOOmail (especially in text-only MOO clients) is to type the whole message itself in the subject field. Although the MOO will happily allow you to do this, you can avoid this mistake by always remembering that the first thing the MOO asks you to input after you have issued the *@send* command is the subject of your message.

After you have entered the subject of your message, you are moved from the room you were in to the mail editor. You are now ready to compose the body of your message. The easiest way to do this is by typing the word *enter,*

```
                            Lingua MOO

@send Cynthia
Subject:
[Type a line of input or `@abort' to abort the command.]
MOOniversity manuscript
Mail Room

Do a 'look' to get the list of commands, or 'help' for assistance.

Composing a letter to Cynthia (#84) entitled "MOOniversity manuscript"
"Hi Cynthia,
Line 1 added.
"Work on the MOOniversity manuscript is going very well, and we should be able
to have a draft ready by tomorrow.
Line 2 added.
"Will get back to you after a return from Norway on April 1st.
Line 3 added.
"Cheers,
Line 4 added.
"Jan
Line 5 added.
send
Sending...
Mail actually sent to Cynthia (#84)
The Studio
```

FIGURE 4.3   A Sample MOOmail Session

followed by pressing the return key (on some keyboards, also called the enter key). This will switch the editor to input mode. You can now compose your message consisting of as many lines as you want. When you are through composing your message, type a single period (.) on a line by itself, and press the return key once more. Your message will now be saved. To send it, simply type *send*, and to exit the mail editor, type *quit*. On exiting the editor, you will be moved back to the room where you were before you started to compose your MOOmail.

Receiving and Reading MOOmail

MOOmails you receive are sent to your MOO mailbox. Notification of new mail is printed immediately on your screen when it is received in your mailbox, or, if you were not logged on when the mail was sent, you will be notified that you have new MOOmail the next time you connect. There are basically two different ways you can read your MOOmail. The first involves opening your mailbox and specifying the message you wish to read; the second will let you read all new messages, both in your mailbox and on MOO mailing lists you are subscribed to (more on this later), in the order they were received.

You open your mailbox with the command *@mail*. This will display the contents of your mailbox, listing old and new messages ordered by the date they were received. Unread messages, if any, are marked with a plus sign (+). To read message number one, for example, you type: @*read 1.* To read message number three, type @*read 3,* and so on.

```
@mail
3 messages:
    1:  Mar 16 10:14  Bitstream (#100)  MOOniversity
>>>2:   Mar 16 15:40  Cynthia (#84)     Player Request
    3:+ Mar 16 21:15  Bitstream (#100)  Re: MOOniversity
----+
```

You can also read new MOOmail using the @*nn* command. Type @*nn* successively to read new messages one by one in the order they were received. The @*nn* command will let you read both personal MOOmail and mail sent to MOO mailing lists you subscribe to. When there is no more new mail to read, you will be notified to this effect.

Managing Your MOOmail

If you are an avid MOOmailer who regularly receives a lot of mail from others, your MOO mailbox will quickly fill up with messages. Although you can have hundreds of messages in your mailbox, it is a good idea to periodically manage your mail by deleting old messages. The command for deleting MOOmail messages is @*rm.* If you enter this command right after having read a MOOmail, it assumes you want to delete the message you just read, and it deletes it. If you don't delete that message right then, later you must specify which message or messages to delete. If, for example, you wish to delete message number two in your mailbox, the syntax is: @*rm 2.* If you wish to delete messages two through six, the syntax is @*rm 2-6,* and if you wish to delete all messages after, say, number three, the correct syntax would be @*rm 3-$.* Note here that the dollar sign is used to signify the last message in your mailbox.

(i)

MOOmail, like everything else that is created or written in the MOO, adds to the size of the MOO itself. Sometimes, if a MOO becomes too big it may actually outgrow the resources of the computer on which it is running. Although it is the MOO administrators' job to make sure that this doesn't happen, you can help a lot by being diligent at deleting old MOOmail messages you no longer need.

After you have deleted a message or a selection of messages from your mailbox, the numbering of messages may be out of order. To fix this, you should always type the command *@renumber* after you have deleted MOO-mail messages.

There are also a number of other ways you can manage your MOOmail, for example, having it automatically forwarded to your Internet e-mail address. To find out more about these other options, please type *help mail-options* while in the MOO.

The enCore Xpress MOO Mailer

If you are using enCore Xpress, you can take advantage of the greatly simplified editing features that this system provides (see Figures 4.4 and 4.5). Sending a MOOmail using this system is as easy as clicking on a button and entering your message. Another advantage is that you can easily edit and make corrections in your message before you send it. Reading MOOmail messages with Xpress is also very simple; just select the mailbox you want, and click on the message you wish to read.

MOO Mailing Lists

The MOO mailing lists, or *newsgroups* as they are also called, are not much different from Internet mailing lists or Usenet newsgroups that you may have used before. Their purpose is to make it easy for people who work on related projects, or who share similar interests, to collaborate and share information. MOO mailing lists can be created for any topic, and in large MOOs there may be more than a hundred of them. Although not every educational MOO uses mailing lists very much (some may not have any at all), most of them do.

To see what mailing lists are available in your MOO, type *@subscribe*. If the MOO has any mailing lists that you can subscribe to, they will be displayed on your screen, as illustrated in Figure 4.6.

①

Note that mailing lists are displayed with an asterisk (*) preceding their name. It is very important that you include this asterisk whenever you refer to a mailing list.

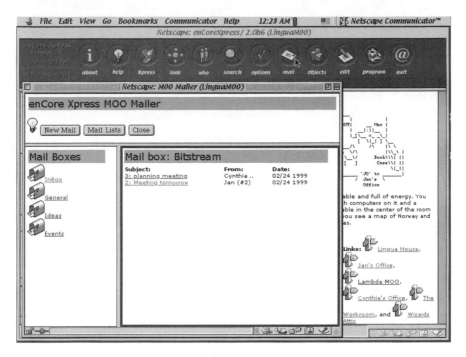

FIGURE 4.4   enCore Xpress MOO Mailer

FIGURE 4.5   Composing and Sending MOOmail with Xpress

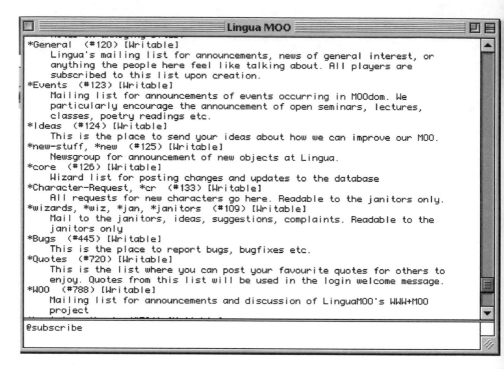

FIGURE 4.6   Selection of Mailing Lists from Lingua MOO

Subscribing and Unsubscribing from Mailing Lists

Mail that is sent to a mailing list is only distributed to those who are *subscribed* to the list, so subscribing to a list is the first thing you need to do. Let's say that your teacher has set up a discussion list for your class called **classlist*. In order to subscribe to this list you would type: *@subscribe *classlist with notification*. If the MOO responds with "I don't understand that," make sure that you typed the name of the list correctly, that you included the asterisk as part of the list's name, and try again. Not all mailing lists are open for subscription by everyone. Some lists may be restricted to, for example, administrators only. If you attempt to subscribe to such a list, the MOO will tell you that the list "is not readable by you." You may subscribe to as many lists as you wish, and typing the command *@subscribed* at any time will show you what lists you are currently subscribed to. Only the MOO administrators may create new mailing lists, so if you are interested in nineteenth-century English literature and would like to have a list where you can discuss this with others, talk to an administrator and ask if they can create such a list for you.

To remove yourself, or unsubscribe from a list, type *@unsubscribe *list-name*. If you wish to unsubscribe from a list called *grammar-discussion, you should type: *@unsubscribe *grammar-discussion*.

Post to a Mailing List

Posting a message to a mailing list is virtually identical to sending a MOO-mail to someone, with the exception that instead of using a person's name, you use the name of the list as the address. To post a message to the class list we mentioned above, for example, you would thus type: *@send *classlist*. Note that you can also send a message to both a mailing list and other users or to several mailing lists. The examples below illustrate this. First we post a message to **classlist* copying Cynthia, and then we send the same message to two different mailing lists.

```
@send *classlist Cynthia
@send *classlist *grammar-discussion
```

(i)

Crossposting to several mailing lists is something that should be done with great caution. A good number of people may be subscribed to all the lists on which you post your message, and they will receive multiple copies of your message. This practice is also called *spamming*, and is generally frowned on.

Reading Posts on Mailing Lists

If there is new mail on any of the lists you are subscribed to, you will be notified with a message on your screen to that effect, or the next time you log on to the MOO. Unlike personal MOOmail, however, which is stored in your own private MOO mailbox, mailing list mail is stored on the list itself. This means that you can be subscribed to as many lists as you want without fearing that the messages will take up a lot of database space. It also means that mail from a mailing list will not show up in your mailbox. To read this mail you can either use the *@nn* command described above, or use the *@read* command to access mail on specific lists. The general format for reading mail on mailing lists is *@read message on *mail-list*. For example, to read message number two on **classlist* you would type: *@read 2 on *classlist*. If you don't know the number of a message, you can start backwards by reading the last message on the list by typing *@read last on *classlist*. Once you have read a message on a list, you can read the previous or the next message on that list using the following commands:

```
@read prev on *classlist
@read next on *classlist
```

Managing Mailing Lists the Xpress Way

enCore Xpress provides an easier way to manage your mail list subscriptions than the traditional way we have just explained. You open the mail list manager by clicking on the *mail list button* in the MOO Mail Editor. In the new window that opens, you'll be presented with a list of available mailing lists in your MOO (Figure 4.7). The lists that you are already subscribed to will be checked. To subscribe to a new list or unsubscribe from a list, you simply select or deselect the lists you want.

The MOO Newspaper

The MOO's newspaper, usually referred to simply as *news*, is the MOO administrators' information channel. In the news you can read about things that involve the MOO and its operation, announcements of various kinds, or simply other information that the administrators want everyone in the MOO to know about.

To see the MOO newspaper's table of contents, type *news* at any time. This command displays a numbered list of news articles on your screen showing the title of each article, who wrote it, and when it was last updated, as illustrated in Figure 4.8. To read a certain article, type *news* followed by the number of the article you wish to read. For example, to read article number five in the newspaper, you would type *news 5*. Articles that you haven't yet read or articles that have been changed or updated since the last time you read them are marked with an asterisk (*) beside their title.

Whenever there is an update to the MOO newspaper, you will be notified about it immediately on your screen. As long as there are articles in the newspaper that you haven't read, a notice will be printed to this effect every time you log on. If you think that you have read all the articles in the newspaper, but are still notified when you log in that there are new articles to read, chances are that one or more articles have been updated since you read them.

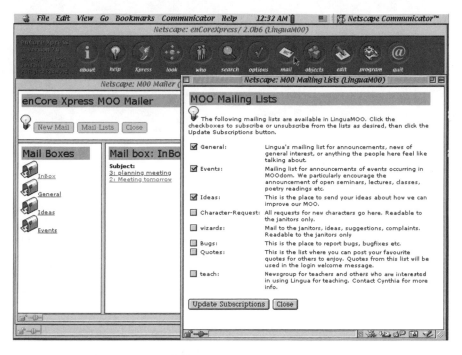

FIGURE 4.7 The Xpress Mail List Manager

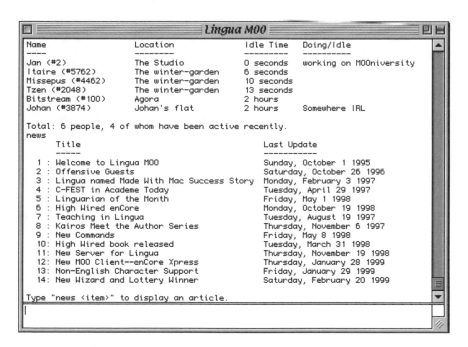

FIGURE 4.8 Sample MOO Newspaper Index

You are advised to read the newspaper whenever there are new articles because they may contain important information from the MOO administrators.

IRC-Style Chat Channels

In MOOs that have them, another way you can communicate with other MOOers online is by using the IRC-style chat channels. Most enCore-based MOOs have the infrastructure necessary to set up such channels, but may not have implemented any. Ask a MOO administrator if channels are available in your MOO.

(i)

IRC stands for Internet Relay Chat, and is a popular way that people can communicate across the Internet.

The MOO Chat Channels may best be described as the synchronous equivalent to mailing lists. However, because the channels are real-time means of communication, what is being said on the channels is not archived as in the case of mailing lists. Any number of channels for a variety of topics may be created, and by subscribing to them you can communicate with other subscribers in real time across rooms and locations in the MOO. In order to use the chat channel system, you must first add the feature called *$channel_FO*. Please see the section on *features* below for information on how to do this.

To subscribe to a channel, first type *@xchannels* to see what channels are available in your MOO. If you see a channel called, for example, Rhetoric Discussion, you can now join that channel with the command *@xconnect Rhetoric Discussion*. To say something to everyone who is listening to the channel you just joined, type *x* followed by one space and then whatever you want to say, and to emote something on a channel, type *x* immediately followed by a colon and then your emote as illustrated below:

```
x Hi, I'm new on this channel
x:smiles and waves to everyone
```

For more information on commands you can use with channels please type *help $channel_FO* whenever you are logged on. Note that the commands will differ in MOOs with other channel systems installed.

Features, What They Are and How to Use Them

Features, or feature objects, are something you will be hearing a lot about in the MOO, so we are going to discuss what they are and how to use them in some detail here. In essence, features are handy collections of verbs or commands that you can use. In many cases MOO programmers will make use of feature objects in order to share with others new commands they write. These commands come in addition to the commands that you already have available to you. Unlike most of the verbs we have discussed thus far, however, commands found on feature objects are not usually immediately available to you. In most cases, you need to *add a feature* to your character before you can use any of the commands it provides.

The command for adding a feature is *@addfeature*. This command takes a feature object that you specify and adds it to your character, thus making the commands on the feature available to you. Let us say that someone has made a feature object called *Juli's Aloha Feature*, which contains some cool verbs for greeting other MOOers. If you want to be able to use these verbs, you must first add the feature to your character by typing *@addfeature Juli's Aloha Feature*.

Because there is usually no way of knowing what features might be available in your MOO, you typically have to find out on your own by checking to see what features others are using. If you want to know what features another user named Britt is using, type *@features for Britt*. If Britt is using any features at all, a list of her features will be displayed. To find out how a certain feature works, you need to use its object number and type *help feature-object-number* (sometimes players program a feature object and do not include a help text, so this does not always give you information). You can now use the *@addfeature* command to add the feature objects you want to your own character. Note that in this case you need to refer to the feature by its object number because usually you are neither in the same room as the feature object, nor would you be holding it. To find out what features you are using, you can simply type *@features*. Features can also be removed at any time by typing *@rmfeature feature-name* or *number*, for example, *@rmfeature #112*.

In enCore-based MOOs, characters start out with a base set of features already installed. These features are the social verbs feature, the login watching feature, and the pasting feature.

The Social Verbs Feature

This is a feature object consisting of a great number of preprogrammed emotes that you can use in various social situations. Instead of emoting, you can use these preprogrammed emotes simply by typing their name. For example, *smile*. To smile to someone specific, you can type *smile person*. For example, *smile Jan*. You can see the whole list of these social verbs below. Online, type *feelings* at any time to see the same list:

comfort	poke	laugh	brb
wink	shrug	sigh	grin
yawn	blush	chuckle	clap
wave	cringe	hug	cheer
cackle	smirk	kiss	pine
giggle	nod	bow	froll
cry	smile	vnod	lei
bounce	snuggle	claugh	pout
cuddle	tackle	purr	gasp
curtsey	tickle	brow	thwap
hkiss	wiggle	booga	groan
highf	cgrin	xgrin	mgroan
ruffle	salute	wait	moan
shiver	boot	tap	amoan
note	manner	phone	afk
pnote	dictionary	visitor	ok
hmm	list	sync	lag

The Login Watcher

This is a useful feature that will tell you whenever someone logs on or off from the MOO. You switch it on and off by typing *@login*.

The Pasting Feature

This is a highly useful feature that enables you to paste text from various sources into the MOO so others can read it. In order to use this feature you must use a client program that supports cut and paste. For an example of the usefulness of the pasting feature, let's say that you are having a discussion with your teacher about a paper. At some point in the discussion you may want to show your teacher an excerpt from your paper. Instead of having to type in the text you want your teacher to see, you can simply paste it into your MOO window. Here's one way you can do it.

Open your word processing program with the file that contains your paper and select (or highlight) the paragraph (by dragging the mouse pointer over it) you wish to show your teacher. Copy the paragraph using the copy function in your word processing program. Switch to your MOO client program window and type *@paste*. Next, paste in the paragraph you copied using your MOO client's paste function. Finally, type a period (.) on a line by itself and press the return (or enter) key. The text you pasted in will now be displayed on the screens of everyone in the room. If you wish to paste something to only one person, use *@pasteto name* instead of *@paste* above.

Privacy and Safety

Before we conclude this chapter, we want to mention a few things concerning privacy and safety in the MOO. No matter how hard the MOO administrators work to prevent harassment, occasionally it becomes a problem. Although it is not extremely likely that something like this might actually happen to you, you should know how to deal with it and protect yourself if it should ever become a problem.

Your first line of defense should always be to talk to the person you are having trouble with and tell them to stop whatever they are doing. Oftentimes, this is all it takes to solve the problem. If this doesn't help, you can use the *@gag person* command, which will effectively filter out anything the person says, does, or pages until you type *@ungag person*. You can also contact one of the MOO administrators for help. To find out if any of them are online, type *@wizards*. If no administrators happen to be online, type *help wizard-list* to see the names of all administrators in the MOO. If you are using a client program that enables you to log your MOO session, we recommend that you start a log in order to capture what the person is saying and doing. This might be important evidence later if the other person refuses any knowledge of the situation.

If you are in a room you own (see Chapter 6 for more on how to build your own rooms), you can use the command *@eject! person* to kick out folks who are bothering you. If you are forced to do this, we recommend that you lock your room with the following command *@lock here with me* so that the perpetrator cannot reenter your room. Don't forget to unlock your room with *@unlock here* later so other people can come in. That can be disconcerting for your friend or teacher who knocks on your virtual door, receives your invitation to join you, and can't get in! They would see:

```
@join cynthia
Sorry, you can't go there.
```

As you can see, becoming a MOO Citizen is quite like RL, but in fast motion! The fun part is that *you* get to decide how you "appear" to others, and *you* get to customize your persona, your messages, and your features. Just as writing in class for exams or essays is important to how you communicate your ideas, so are the kinds of writing that construct your online world. You are, in effect, communicating everything in writing. Virtual literacy is about much more than becoming literate about computer commands and software.

Writing takes on an existential responsibility. Your writing is who, where, when, why, and how you are on the MOO.

CLASS DISCUSSION

1. As a class, discuss how player descriptions inform perceptions of identity and how the textual representation of surroundings reflects on the notion of situatedness in MOOs in general, and in specific MOOs that your teacher assigns you to visit. In other words, discuss how the textual variables you read alter your understanding of identity (both your own and others you interact with).

2. Discuss the various player classes and how the gaming origins affect MOO as a learning environment. That is, distinguish between dedicated writing environment programs (if you have had experience with Daedalus Interchange and other DIWE software), IRC-chat channels, and MOOs where students themselves are allowed to design and extend the space as well as interact there. Do you think that adds to the learning environment? If so, why?

3. Emotes are not the typical way we talk about actions and feelings, but in the MOO they become extremely important modes of communication. We're not talking here about emoticons (those little smiley faces), though you can certainly use those to communicate feelings as well. As a class, and IRL, take turns standing at your seat and speak your emotes to the class, just as you would have typed your feelings or actions in the MOO. For example, if you want to smile or wave, stand up and say out loud, "Mike smiles sheepishly." Or perhaps, say, "Jennifer waves wildly to get the teacher's attention!" Now, everyone try this at once, and you'll get the feel for using language to emote, and for listening to everyone at once. Granted, in the MOO, conversations follow some sense of order because you can read each line sequentially, but it is often out of the order in which people would normally speak in turn, and to specific others in the room. Learning to emote in language is fun and challenging!

EXERCISES

1. Apply for a character at a MOO (either one you have been assigned to use in your class and/or one of your choice), and be sure to look for the character request policy, usually available by typing *help request:*

```
help request
Showing help on '@request-character':
----
Usage: @request <player-name> for <email-address>
```

```
This command available to Guest characters only. The @request
command requests a new character, registered for your e-mail
address. Please use your primary address for this, as your
password will be sent to the address provided.
```

2. Log on to the MOO of choice (either as a guest or as a player you have now acquired) and set your description. Be creative, but not offensive! Use your MOO notebook to draft your description before you enter it online.

3. Look up the gender options at the MOO and set your gender preference. You might want to try out some of the options and interact with other players in order to experiment with how gender perceptions affect online interaction.

4. Some of your class members log on to the MOO anonymously, choosing names with which the rest of the class cannot determine their identity. The other class members log on as who they "really" are. What advantages and disadvantages do you see about anonymity? Make notes and then do the experiment in the reverse and compare experiences.

5. Practice sending MOOmail by following the instructions in this chapter. Send a mail message to your teacher and one to any other student in your class.

6. Subscribe to a MOO mailing list, either your class list, or one available for special interest groups on that MOO. Don't forget to find out first what lists are available to subscribe to.

7. Add some features to your character, if you have one (guests may not add features as a rule). Explore other features available by looking at features that other players use. Test each command on the feature to see how it works.

8. Practice using the paste feature with your peer critique group (or teacher). You can start by opening up a word file (preferably one that you are working on, such as an essay for class) and copying and pasting a paragraph into the MOO for others to see. Make notes in your MOO notebook about ways to use the paste feature for peer critiques, collaboration, group research, and so forth.

5 The MOO Editors and How to Use Them

In the MOO there are three different *editors* you will probably encounter at one point or another: the *mail editor* (used for composing and sending MOO-mail messages to other MOO users); the *text editor* (used to enter and edit textual descriptions and other object property values); and the *verb editor* (used by programmers to write and compile MOO verbs). Because all three editors are essentially alike and work in similar ways, we cover them together in this chapter.

(i)

One interesting side note about using the MOO editors: Whenever you invoke an editor (whether the mail, text, or verb editor), your character actually leaves the room you are in and enters the editor "room." Those in the same room are notified to this effect:

> A small swarm of 3 × 5 index cards arrives, engulfs Allison, and carries her away.

When you finish editing, they will see something like this:

> A small swarm of 3 × 5 index cards blows in and disperses, revealing Allison.

You may sometimes notice players in the @*who* listing whose location also says [mailing], [editing verbs], or [editing notes]. While you are editing you can receive pages and send pages to other players. This will not affect the editing you are working on, so don't worry. (This is not the case with the Xpress mail editor. A separate window opens that allows you to remain interactive.)

The first thing that you will notice about the MOO editors is that they are quite different from the WYSIWYG-type (What You See Is What You Get) word processing programs and text editors that you normally use on your Macintosh or Windows computer. Because all communication in MOOs happens sequentially line by line, the MOO editors are also line-oriented. Those of you who happen to be familiar with the line editor *vi* in the UNIX operating system will feel right at home with the MOO editors. Because of the line-oriented way the MOO editors force you to specify exactly what line in a text you wish to type on, and precisely what word or words you wish to edit before you are allowed to enter or edit any text, they may at first glance seem hard to use and not very user-friendly. Once you learn to use them, however, you will discover that, despite this little nuisance, they are in fact quite powerful and will always help you get the job done.

The MOO editors are fairly well documented in the help system, and you are well advised to spend some time familiarizing yourself with these help texts. Typing the command *look* whenever you are in an editor will produce an overview of editor-specific commands on your screen (Figure 5.1)

Text Input

There are basically two different ways you can enter text in a MOO editor. The first method is to enter text line by line using the *say command*. The second is to use the *enter function* that we mentioned in Chapter 4.

```
┌──────────────────────── Lingua MOO ────────────────────────┐
look
Note Editor
Commands:

say            <text>                    w*hat
emote          <text>                    mode        [string|list]
lis*t          [<range>] [nonum]         e*dit       <note>
ins*ert        [<ins>] ["<text>]         save        [<note>]
n*ext,p*rev    [n] ["<text>]             abort
enter                                    q*uit,done,pause
del*ete        [<range>]
f*ind          /<str>[/[c][<range>]]
s*ubst         /<str1>/<str2>[/[g][c][<range>]]
m*ove,c*opy    [<range>] to <ins>
join*l         [<range>]
fill           [<range>] [@<col>]

----   Do `help <cmdname>' for help with a given command.   ----

  <ins>   ::= $ (the end) | [^]n (above line n) | _n (below line n) | . (current)
  <range> ::= <lin> | <lin>-<lin> | from <lin> | to <lin> | from <lin> to <lin>
    <lin> ::= n | [n]$ (n from the end) | [n]_ (n before .) | [n]^ (n after .)
  `help insert' and `help ranges' describe these in detail.
```

FIGURE 5.1 Note Editor Commands

The *Say* Command

This is actually the same command that you use in order to talk to other people, except that, in the context of the MOO editor, you "speak" to the editor itself. To enter a line of text, you type *say*, or alternatively a double quotation mark ("), followed by the text you wish to enter. An example illustrates how this command is used to input text. (Note that the MOO always confirms that a line has been added.)

```
say Hi Victor, The work on MOOniversity is going very well.
Line 1 added.
say It's very inspiring to be out here at Ghost Ranch, New
Mexico writing this book, even though we don't have Internet
access here.
Line 2 added.
say Cheers, Cynthia and Jan
Line 3 added
```

The *Enter* Function

Another very useful way to enter text into a MOO editor is by way of the *enter function*. This method will let you type text without having to precede every line with the word *say*, and, even better, it will let you paste in text from virtually any other source, such as your word processing program or a Web page.

- You switch the MOO editor to input mode by typing the word *enter* and hitting the return key (on some keyboards, also called the enter key). You can now compose your text consisting of as many lines as you want.
- When you are through composing your message, type a single period (.) on a line by itself and hit the return key once more.
- To paste in text from an external source, such as a file in your word processing program, first open the MOO editor you wish to use for the mail, text, or verb you wish to edit and type *enter*. Then open the file that contains the text you wish to paste in and select the text by highlighting it (drag your mouse over the text while holding down the mouse button). Next, copy this text using the copy function in your word processing program, which on most systems is found under the edit menu. Switch back to your MOO client program, and choose paste from your client program's edit menu. The text you have selected will now be pasted into the MOO editor.
- To exit input mode and return to normal editor operations, type a period on a line by itself, and hit the return key.
- To save your editing, type the word *save*, then the word *quit* to exit the editor.

The following example illustrates how this procedure looks if you are editing a note that you have created. (The responses from the MOO are boldfaced.)

```
@notedit sign.text
```
Now editing "sign"(#3045).
```
enter
```
[Type lines of input; use '.' to end or '@abort' to abort the command.]
```
Welcome to our studio. Please make yourself at home and feel
free to browse the notes and other help materials you see
here.
     If we are not online you can leave us a MOO mail, or come
back to see us later.

Cheers, Cynthia and Jan
.
```
Lines 1-4 added.
```
save
quit
```

The *List* Command: Viewing the Editor's Contents

You can always see the contents of the mail, text, or verb you are working on by typing the command *list*. Usually, this lists out the last twenty lines of the text you are editing, or up to twenty-four lines of text on the screen if your lines are longer than seventy-nine characters.

In order to list specific sections of the text, you can give two line numbers as an interval argument to the list command. For example, if you wish to see the first three lines of the text, type: list 1-3

In the MOO editors, the dollar sign ($) is used to denote the last line in a text, so in order to list the whole text you can type:

```
list 1-$
1: Welcome to our studio. Please make yourself at home and
feel free to browse the notes and other help materials you
see here.
     2: If we are not online you can leave us a MOO mail, or
come back to see us later
     3:
__4_ Cheers, Cynthia and Jan
^^^^
```

The *Insert* Command: Changing the Insertion Point

Whenever you start a MOO editing session, the insertion point, or the place in the text where you start typing, is always just below the last line. If you are working on a mail, text, or verb that doesn't contain any text yet, this basically means that you start on the first line since there is no last line yet. In many cases, you either want to insert new lines into a mail, text, or verb or change words or phrases in the text. In order to do this, you must first move the insertion point to where you want to insert or edit the text. To accomplish this, use the *insert command,* and specify the number of the line to which you want to move the insertion point. When you use the insert command, the MOO assumes that, unless otherwise stated, you want to move the insertion point to the line just above the line you specify, so, for example, in order to move the insertion point between lines four and five in a text, you should type:

```
insert 5
```

If you want to move the insertion point below a line, for example, if you have previously moved it up and now want to move it back below the last line, you need to precede the line number in the insert command with an underscore:

```
insert _6
```

This command moves the insertion point below line six, whereas the following command moves it below the last line in the text:

```
insert _$
```

The *Substitute* Command: Editing Text with the MOO Editors

In order to change a word, sentence, or phrase using the MOO editors, you need to use the *substitute command,* which is normally shortened to just *s.* Because the MOO editors are line-oriented, as we explained earlier, you need to specify both what text you wish to substitute, and in which line the text occurs. Let's say that we have misspelled the word *Macintosh* in line five of a text we are working on. To change *makintosh* to *Macintosh* using the substitute command, you need to type:

```
s /makintosh/Macintosh/5
```

What this command tells the MOO is to find a word in line five that matches the pattern "makintosh" and replace it with the word *Macintosh*.

The substitute commands always replace the first occurrence of a word, so if you wish to change, say, a period to a comma in a line with more than one period, you must expand the search pattern so that it uniquely points to the period you want to replace. For example, consider the following line, which we have decided to split:

```
The Apple Macintosh, introduced in 1984, was the first
personal computer with a graphical user interface, and for
this reason, it quickly became very popular in schools and
universities.
```

It happens to be line seven in the text we are working on, so we split it into two sentences by replacing the third comma with a period, deleting the word *and* directly following that comma, and finally capitalizing the word *for* that follows thereafter. All this can easily be accomplished with the following substitute command:

```
s /, and f/. F/7
```

Note that the search pattern must match exactly the text you wish to replace, otherwise the MOO will tell you that it cannot find the text you wish to replace. Using the substitute command can be very helpful if you need to fix small typos and errors in your mail messages, texts, or verbs. But in most cases, editing is best done either offline, which we will return to shortly, or by using the enCore Xpress editors that we'll talk about more in the following chapters.

The *Move* and *Copy* Commands

You can move or copy a line or lines from one point in your text to another by using the *move* and *copy* commands. To use these commands you must specify what line or lines you want to move or copy and where you want to move or copy them. If you wish to move, let's say, line seven in a text you are working on up to a point between lines three and four, you type:

```
move 7 to 4
```

To move several lines, for example, lines seven through nine, to the same position, type:

```
move 7-9 to 4
```

To copy the lines used in the examples above, type:

```
copy 7 to 4
copy 7-9 to 4
```

For more information about these and other commands you can use in the MOO editors, type *look* and *help commands* while in an editor, then type *help command-name* for detailed information about a specific command. In the following, we outline the main differences between how you invoke the three different editors, and how you mail or save your work when you are through.

The Mail Editor

You enter the mail editor with the command *@send*. As explained in Chapter 4, this command takes the name or names of MOO users or mailing lists as arguments. Type the command *send* to send the MOOmail.

```
@send person
Enter/edit mail message
send
quit
```

The Text Editor

To invoke the text editor you type *@notedit* followed by the object and the property you wish to edit. You separate the object's name or number from the property name by a period. Type the word *save* to save the text or property value, and the word *quit* to end the editing session.

```
@notedit object.property
Enter/edit property value
save
quit
```

The Verb Editor

You invoke the verb editor by typing *@edit* followed by the object and the verb you wish to edit. Note that the object's name or number should be separated from the verb name by a colon. Type the command *compile* to compile and save your verb and the word *quit* to end the editing session.

```
@edit object:verb
Enter/edit verb program
compile
quit
```

Offline Editing Strategies

Preparing and editing your mail messages, texts, and verbs offline using your favorite text editor or word processor is a good strategy to avoid dealing with the often troublesome and time-consuming task of editing text using the MOO editors. As we have explained above, text that you prepare offline can easily be transferred to the MOO and saved there by using the *enter* function. Another reason why offline editing is a good idea is that work you do online on the MOO may in some cases get lost if the MOO server crashes. Although the MOO makes a complete backup of itself, usually once every hour (in some large MOOs, backups may only be taken once every twelve or twenty-four hours), there is always a risk that a server crash may happen before a backup of your most recent work is taken. If you make it a habit to always create and edit your MOO texts and verbs offline, saving them on your hard disk or a floppy disk, and using the *enter* function to transfer them to the MOO, you will not risk losing your work if the MOO should crash.

The MOO editors are a bit challenging at first, but be assured that with a little practice (as with any new software) you will be editing with ease in no time.

EXERCISES

1. Set up a special section in your MOO notebook for questions, notes, and short-cuts to use in the MOO editors. You may find it useful to print out the MOO editor help texts and attach them to your notebook section on editors.

2. Practice offline editing by revising your player description in a word file, then revise it in the MOO through *@notedit,* copying and pasting your new description in where your old one was.

3. Practice revising your room description using the same process, first offline editing, then MOO editing.

4. Practice the substitution, insertion, and move functions by line-editing one of your texts or descriptions. Copy and paste the editing session into a file you can print and attach in your MOO notebook. (This will come in handy in the future.)

6 Digging in the MUD: How to Create Rooms and Other Objects

The ability to add to the MOOniverse by writing new spaces is one of the most powerful and intriguing features of the MOO technology. As we have said in various ways throughout the book, virtual literacy opens up the possibility for viewing writing in new ways, for using writing in new ways, and for evaluating writing in new ways. It may seem odd to think of MOO building (Chapter 6) and MOO programming (Chapter 7) as writing, much less as writing that earns you a grade. We think that the proliferation of educational MOOs and research about their effects on learning is radically altering our view of what counts as writing, but most of all as "good" writing. Chances are that if you are using *MOOniversity*, your teacher understands and shares these new perceptions about writing, thinking, reading, and interacting via synchronous textual learning environments like educational MOOs.

In this chapter we talk about how you can build a room for yourself in cyberspace and create interactive objects of all sorts. The various building tools that you will be using are discussed in detail along with examples of how to use both the basic and more advanced building features that the MOO can offer.

How to Become a Builder

You learned in Chapter 4 that in order to use the building features the MOO has to offer, your character must be a *builder*. If you don't have builder status, request it from a MOO administrator. Some MOO administrators give users builder status automatically, while others require you to apply by asking why you wish to be a builder and what you plan to create.

The Dynamics of MOO Creation

Because of its *object-oriented nature,* building is quite easy in the MOO. We will turn to a more thorough discussion of the object-orientation of MOOs in the chapter on programming, but for now let's just say that because the MOO is object-oriented, you build and create things based on blueprints or templates that already exist in the MOO. These blueprints are called *classes* or *generic objects,* and you use them as *parents* for your new creations. What this means is that you don't have to start from scratch every time you want to build something; instead, you make a new instance of an already existing generic object and customize it by giving it a new description and so on.

Generic Classes and Objects

Every object in the MOO can, in principle, be used as a blueprint for new objects, but certain specially programmed objects have been designated as generic classes, meaning that everyone can use them as blueprints for their own creations. Every MOO has a core set of these generic classes. These are the generic room, the generic thing, the generic container, the generic note, and the generic letter. The generic letter is actually just a refinement of the generic note that allows you to create personalized (encrypted) letters that only the person or persons that you designate can read.

(!)

These core classes can also be referred to by preceding their name with a dollar sign like this: *$room, $thing, $container, $note,* and *$letter* (see Figure 6.1).

All of this will become more evident as we go into some detailed examples later in this chapter of how object-oriented principles work in practical terms.

(i)

In the MOO all things are objects, and all are derived from a base set of classes. Even your own character is an object that is based on a special class called *$player.* When your character is "upgraded" to builder, what really happens is that the MOO administrators change your parent class from *$player* to *$builder.* Similarly, if you become a programmer, your parent class is changed to *$programmer.*

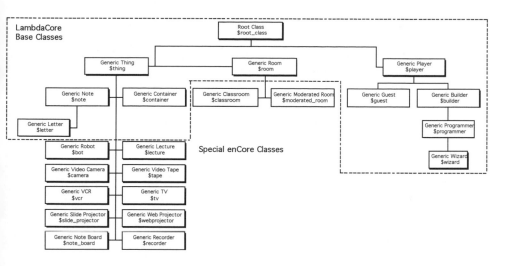

FIGURE 6.1   LambdaCore Base Class Hierarchy

Creating Your Own MOOspace: How to Use the *@dig* Command

The two most frequently used commands in every MOO builder's toolbox are *@dig* and *@create*. The *@dig* command is used to build new rooms and exits, whereas *@create* is used as a general construction tool to create any type of MOO object.

The *@dig* command has been carried over from the early days of MUD and refers to the process of digging new caves in the virtual dungeon.

The first thing people usually want to create in a MOO is a room. In its simplest form, the *@dig* command creates a room based on the generic class, *$room,* and gives it a name that you specify. You must type the name you wish to call your new room directly following the *@dig* command. In technical terms, we say that you give the name of your new room as an *argument* to the *@dig* command.

```
@dig Study
Study (#100) created.
```

In response to this command, the MOO creates a new room named Study. When you use this simple form of @*dig*, your new room is not being connected to the rest of the MOO; it is simply being placed in the *void*, or what is called *Nowhere* in particular. In order to get to it and continue building exits and other objects, therefore, you must teleport to it with the @*go* command that we discussed in Chapter 3. Note here that you must use your new room's object number (the MOO will tell you this number when you make the room) as an argument with @*go* in order to get there.

```
@go #100
You teleport into Study
```

Welcome to your new home in the MOO! As you will discover, it's not really much of a home yet because it's basically just a blueprint of the standard generic room, lacking a good description and other things, but it does have the functionality that all MOO rooms have. What you should do now is get out your textual paint buckets and wallpaper and start decorating and describing your new room with words using the @*describe* command that we talked about in Chapter 3, or the MOO's text editor that we discussed in Chapter 5. To enter a short description using @*describe*, type @*describe here as "You see a small cozy room…"*, and so forth. To enter a longer and textually richer description using the MOO's text editor, type @*notedit here*. If you want a long and detailed description that you think you may want to edit or change later, it might be a good idea to write the description offline and transfer it to the MOO using the text editor's *enter* function as below (see Chapter 5 for more about text editors):

```
@notedit here
Note Editor

Do a 'look' to get the list of commands, or 'help' for
assistance.

Now editing "Study"(#100).description.
enter
[Type lines of input; use '.' to end or '@abort' to abort
the command.]
You enter an office that is comfortable and full of energy.
You see a *worktable with two Macintosh computers on it and
a bookcase. On one wall you see a map of Norway and on the
opposite wall a map of *Texas.
.
Line 1 added.
save
Text written to "Study"(#100).description.
quit
```

In this case, the actual description has been pasted in from a word processor file (or some other program) after the prompt to type lines of input. Once you paste the text in, you type a period on a line by itself (as instructed), and then you type the word *save*, then the word *quit*.

You can, if you wish, designate your new room to be your default starting point (or home) whenever you log in, by typing *@sethome* while being in your room.

Exits

For people to be able to move around in the MOO, rooms and locations must be linked to one another. These links between rooms are called *exits*, and they are also created with the *@dig* command. To illustrate how *@dig* is used to make both rooms and exits, consider the following example. Let's say that you wish to make another room off of your study called Closet, where you can store things. You want to be able to move between the study and the closet via a door in such a way that typing *in* will take you from the study to the closet, and typing *out* will take you back to the study. (See Chapter 3 for more on movement via exits.) To build this closet you use the following arguments with *@dig:*

```
@dig in|out to Closet
```

Note that even though the notion of a door creates the illusion that there is only one exit leading both in and out, there are two exits, *in* and *out*, which together make up the illusion of a door. You can, however, create one-way doors by typing:

```
@dig in to Closet
```

We do not generally recommend that you create one-way exits unless there is a special reason for it (e.g., a trapdoor that one can fall through, but not get back through). If you have no special reason for an exit leading back, then this may create confusion.

(i)

When you create exits between your rooms, it's a good practice to give exits leading back toward your main room the name *out*. This way, if someone gets lost while exploring your MOO rooms, they can type *out* repeatedly until they get back to your main room or starting point.

The *@dig* command can also be used to create exits or passageways between rooms that already exist but were not previously connected. Let's say that you have another room called Attic with object number #1998, and you wish to connect it to your study via two exits called *up* and *down.* You can accomplish this with the command line:

```
@dig up|down to #1998
```

Just as in the first example above, you have now linked the two rooms by making two new exits; only this time no new room is created because the room you connect to, Attic, that has object number #1998, already exists. (See the section on *@audit* later in this chapter for more on how to find out object numbers for rooms and other objects.)

You can't use the name of the room, Attic, instead of its object number when linking to it. You can only refer to an object by its name if you are (1) holding it, or (2) in the room where the object is. In all other cases, you must use the object's number when referring to it.

Connecting Your Rooms to the Rest of the MOO

At some point you may want to connect your rooms to the rest of the MOO so that people may find them easier. You can only connect rooms that you own. So if you try to link to some room that someone else owns, the exits will be created, but the exit leading back to your room will not be functional until the owner of the room you linked to makes it a legal exit from his or her room. In other words, you must first create the two exits using the *@dig* command, then contact the owner of the room you linked to and ask him or her to type *@add-exit* using the object number of the exit leading to your room as an argument. For example, if the number of the exit leading back to your room is #3005, the command should be *@add-exit #3005.*

Many MOOs have specially designated areas where people can connect their rooms, so be sure to ask a MOO administrator before you connect it to the rest of the MOOniverse. Also, please note that it is not polite to link to someone else's room unless he or she has given you explicit permission to do so.

Exit Messages

For every exit you make, you can specify a set of messages that the MOO will display when someone uses the exit. For example, if you have created a doorway called *mouse hole* that is so low and narrow that people must crawl to get through it, you can set the message that is printed when someone comes in through the door to something like "Michael comes crawling through the mouse hole." Setting exit messages in this manner will certainly enhance your MOOspace and make it more interesting for visitors to explore your rooms. When you type *help messages* for further information on messages and how to set them, you will see information like the following:

```
To set a particular message on one of your objects use a
command with this form:
        @<message-name> <object> is "<message>"
where '<message-name>' is the name of the message being set,
<object> is the name or number of the object on which you
want to set that message, and <message> is the actual text.

For example, consider the 'leave' message on an exit; it is
printed to a player when they successfully use the exit to
leave a room. To set the 'leave' message on the exit 'north'
from the current room, use the command
        @leave north is "You wander in a northerly way out
        of the room."

The following help topics describe the uses of the various
messages available on standard kinds of objects:

container-messages -- the messages on objects that can
contain other objects
exit-messages -- the messages on exit objects
thing-messages -- the messages on objects that can be taken
and dropped
```

Creating Aliases for Rooms and Exits

Although a MOO object such as a room or an exit can only have one official name, they can have as many aliases as you wish. This can often be useful if you want to be able to refer to them using shorter names (or nicknames). Aliases can be added when you first create a room or an exit by typing:

```
@dig up,u|down,d to The Spectacular Balcony,balcony,bal
```

In this example we have created a new room called The Spectacular Balcony with aliases *balcony* and *bal*, an exit leading there called *up* with alias *u*, and another exit leading back called *down* with alias *d*.

Aliases may also be added or removed at any later time using the *@add-alias* and *@rmalias* commands. (Consult the in-MOO help system for more information on how to use these commands.)

Creating Other Objects

As we mentioned in the beginning of this chapter, because the MOO is an object-oriented environment, building happens by creating an object from existing generic objects and classes, and then customizing the new instance of the generic object.

When you wish to create something in the MOO, you must always base it on something that already exists. Recall that we mentioned that in every MOO there is a core set of generic objects or classes, *$room* (which we have already used with *@dig* above), *$thing, $container, $note,* and *$letter,* that you can use as blueprints for your own creations. Each of these classes is so general that you can use them to create just about anything you want. Yet, they all have the characteristics of the type of object they represent. For example, the class *$thing* has characteristics of all things in that it has a description and can be picked up and dropped. The class *$container,* which is based on *$thing,* can, in addition, be opened and closed, as well as be used as a storage place for other objects. The class *$note,* which is also based on *$thing,* can be written on and read just as you would expect a note to behave. The class *$letter,* which is based on *$note,* has all the characteristics of a note, but, in addition, it can be used for private communication as you would expect in a letter.

In addition to these five core classes, most MOOs will sport a host of other generic classes on which you can base your objects. For example, MOOs based on the enCore database have at least the following additional classes: Recording and Intercom System (*$recording_system*), Moderated Room (*$moderated_room*), Classroom (*$classroom*), Bot (*$bot*), Slide Projector (*$slide_projector*), Video Camera (*$camera*), VCR (*$vcr*), TV (*$tv*), Video Tape (*$tape*), Recitable Note (*$recitable_note*), Lecture (*$lecture*), Web Page (*$webpage*), Web Projector (*$webprojector*), Recorder and Player (*$recorder*), Note Board (*$note_board*), a World Wide Web client (*$web_slate*), and more. Just as the five core classes above, these additional generic classes have already been programmed with a certain functionality that mimics the things from the physical world that they are supposed to represent. For example, the generic recorder has been programmed to record and log what is being said and done in a room. Thus, in an enCore-based MOO, you can easily get a recorder without having to do any programming yourself. You simply make a new object based on the generic recorder.

To illustrate exactly how the *@create* command is used, let's say that you want to create a sign in your room that other people can read. For this purpose you can use the class *$thing* as your blueprint, and to create the sign you would type the command:

```
@create $thing named Welcome Sign, sign
```

What the command does is tell the MOO to create a new object based on the class $thing, and give it the name "Welcome Sign" with alias "sign." Because the new sign is basically just a blueprint of the generic thing, you should now customize it by giving it a description. As an example, you could type the following description:

```
@describe sign as "You see a wooden sign hanging on the
wall. It reads: Welcome to my room. Please make yourself at
home, and feel free to look around."
```

Whenever visitors look at your sign, they will now be able to read the description you just gave it.

Every time you create a new object, it is placed in your character's inventory; that is, it is assumed that you are holding the object. So, for other people to actually be able to see your sign, you must first drop it in your room. Type *drop sign.*

Let us consider another example. As you proceed to furnish your room, you may want to create a bookshelf that you can put your books and other stuff in. For this purpose, you can use the generic container as the blueprint, and create your bookshelf by typing:

```
@create $container named Book Shelf, shelf.
```

In these two examples, we have illustrated the standard *@create* format that you always use every time you wish to create a new object. First type *@create,* then specify which generic class you wish to use as a blueprint, then tell the MOO what name and eventual aliases you wish to give the new object.

In enCore-based MOO's, you can easily create new objects by simply typing *@create* and then hitting the return key. This will bring up a menu of the most popular classes that you can base your new object on (see Figure 6.2).

The enCore Xpress Object Editor

ⓔ

The enCore Xpress object editor (Figure 6.3) was designed specifically to make it easy to assert your creative side in the MOO. Through its intuitive graphical interface, the click of a button is all it takes to edit objects you own or create new objects and rooms.

You open the Xpress Object Editor by clicking on the Objects button in your Xpress toolbar. To edit an existing object you can either type the name or object number of the object in the search field, or click on the List Objects button. When you have found the object you want to work with, simply click the Edit Object button and start editing. Don't forget to save changes you have made before you leave the object editor.

If you want to create a new object or a room, click on the Create Object button, and a list of available generic classes (blueprints) will appear in the left object editor area. Browse the list until you find the type of object you wish to create and click on it. You will then be asked to name the new object, and, if it is a room, decide where you want to connect it, and what you want to call the entrance and exit. When you have done this you can proceed to edit the new object in the simple manner we have just described.

How to Lock Your Objects

Oftentimes, you may wish to have private conversations with someone and you do not want others to be able to enter your room. Or you may want to prevent others from picking up and walking off with your objects (whether by accident or not). To accomplish this, you can *lock* your room or objects. The general command for locking any object is *@lock object with key*. The key, in this case, is another object that will allow anyone who is carrying it to either enter a room or pick up an object that has been locked with that object as the key. For example, if you wish to lock your room so that no one else but you can enter it, you should type:

```
@lock here with me
```

In this case you tell the MOO to lock your room (*here* always refer to your current location) using yourself as the key. If you wish to prevent others from being able to pick up your sign, you could type:

```
@lock sign with me
```

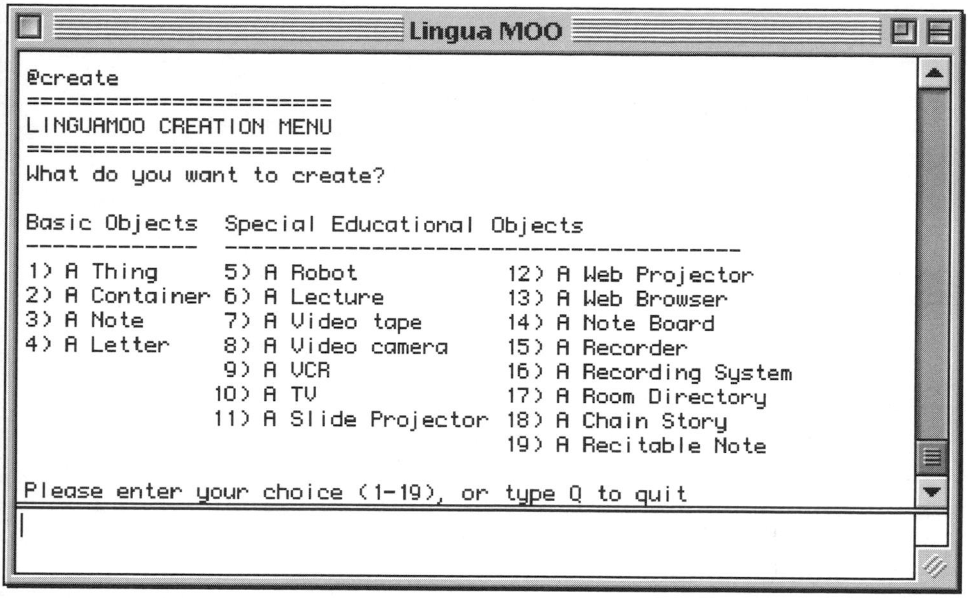

FIGURE 6.2 High Wired enCore Object Creation Menu

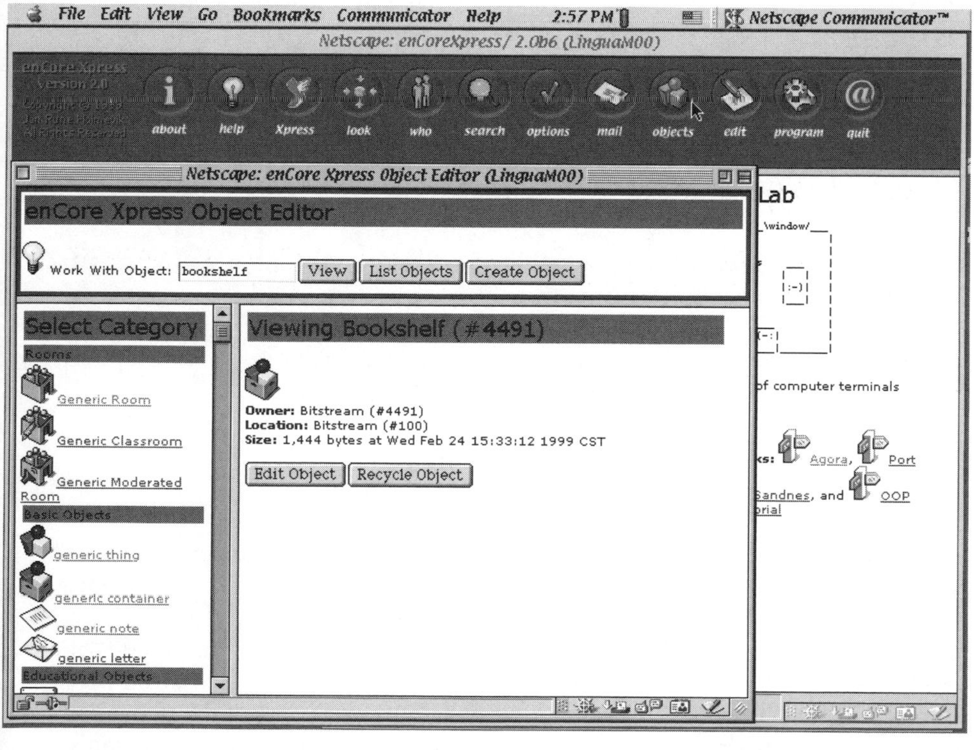

FIGURE 6.3 enCore Xpress Object Editor

You can use any object as a key. Imagine that you have an object called "Golden Key" that you wish to use to lock your room. The format of the *@lock* command would in this case be:

```
@lock here with Golden Key
```

Now, only the person carrying the Golden Key object will be able to enter your room.

To unlock an object, you type *@unlock object*. To open your room to visitors after it's been locked, you should type:

```
@unlock here
```

Note that you will only be able to lock and unlock objects that you yourself own.

Keeping Track of Your Stuff: *@audit*

You can easily find out what you have created by using the command *@audit*. Typing this command without any arguments will produce a list of objects you own with their object numbers, names, and their exact location in the MOO. If you need to know the number of an object you own, as in the example where you created exits between two existing rooms, typing *@audit* is the best way to find out. If you have forgotten to lock an object, and you find that someone has inadvertently walked off with it, you can use *@audit* to locate it. Then make a note of the object's number (obj#) and type *@move obj# to here*, or *@move obj# to me*, depending on whether you wish to move it to your current location or your character's inventory.

You can also use the *@audit* command to find out what other people own by using their name or object number as an argument. For example, typing *@audit Jan* will show you a list of all the objects that Jan owns.

Monitoring Your Resource Usage: *@quota*

If every builder or programmer in the MOO were allowed to create as many objects as he or she wanted, the MOO would soon grow to extreme proportions, and, in the worst case scenario, outgrow the resources of the computer on which it runs. To prevent this from happening and to control the growth of the MOO, every user has a certain *quota* that he or she can use to build and program with. There are essentially two different quota systems in use on MOOs today. The original system is called *object-based quota*, where a person's resource usage is monitored by the number of objects that he or she owns. The second system, which is being used by all enCore-based MOOs and many others, is called *byte-based quota*. In this system a person's resource usage is measured by how many bytes their objects occupy. Byte-based quota is generally considered a much more accurate system for keeping track of resource usage, because individual objects may vary considerably in size. For example, in a MOO using object-based quota, a person who owns, let's say, two rooms and two exits linking those rooms may use less than 5,000 bytes, whereas another person who owns four recorder logs of several hundred lines of text each may easily use over 100,000 bytes.

In a MOO with byte-based quota, builders and programmers usually start out with 25,000 to 50,000 bytes, which is normally sufficient to create a couple of rooms and a few other objects. Typing the command *@quota* at any time will display your current quota usage and how much remains. Once your quota is used, the MOO will not allow you to create any more objects, and in this case you can do one of two things. Either recycle some of the things you already own (see below for more about how to do this), or you can contact the MOO administrators and ask if they can raise your quota. In some MOOs you may be required to apply for more quota, and in this case you should be prepared to explain to the administrators what you intend to use the new quota for. Please keep in mind that the MOO administrators have to think about the MOO's overall resource usage when they decide whether to award you more quota, so the better ideas you have about what you wish to create, the better chance you stand of receiving more quota.

(i)

If you use a MOO recorder to log conversations or meetings in the MOO, you should be aware that these logs may get big and thus will take up quite a bit of your quota. It is therefore a good idea to e-mail the log to yourself by typing *@mailme logname* after your meeting is over, and then recycle the object log as described below to free up quota.

(!)

In some cases, if you are creating more than ten new objects over a short period of time, the MOO may tell you that you have exceeded your resource quota even though the *@quota* command may tell you that you still have plenty of free quota. The problem in this case is that, because the MOO only measures the size of newly created objects once every twenty-four hours, it will prevent you from owning more than ten unmeasured objects. To get around this problem, you can measure your newly created objects with the command @*measure new me*. If, after your new objects have been measured, you still have quota left, you can now go ahead and create the additional objects you want.

Keep Your MOO Tidy: @*recycle*

As we mentioned above, sometimes you may have to recycle objects you have created, either because you no longer want them, or in order to free up quota for other objects. In the MOO, this process is accomplished using the @*recycle command*. For example, if you want to get rid of the sign you created earlier, you can easily do this by typing @*recycle sign*.

Because it's quite easy to accidentally recycle other objects instead of the ones you want, either by misspelling their name or otherwise getting them mixed up, the MOO will ask you if you really want to recycle the object. Be sure you are recycling the right object before you answer *yes* to this question, because once an object has been recycled there is no easy way to get it back. If, in the worst case scenario, you happen to accidentally recycle an object you absolutely need, you should talk to the MOO administrators to see if they can possibly restore it for you from a backup of the MOO.

Maps and Other ASCII Art

Many MOOs make use of ASCII graphics and art to enhance the user interface and MOO experience. ASCII maps that depict the layout of a room or series of rooms are especially useful because of the way they visualize the MOOscape and, thus, make it easier for people, especially visitors and new users, to find their way around. Figures 6.4 and 6.5 from Lingua MOO illustrate how ASCII maps can be used in this manner.

Figure 6.4 shows the basic layout of the Library, which is the most important resource center in Lingua MOO, while Figure 6.5 depicts the architecture of the Agora, which is the center where Lingua's online classrooms are located. Note the way that the Agora map is designed to resemble a real three-dimensional space.

ASCII art may also be used as illustrations of other objects (see Figure 6.6). For many people the graphical representation of an object, together with a detailed description of that object, makes it easier to relate to the virtual reality of the MOOspace.

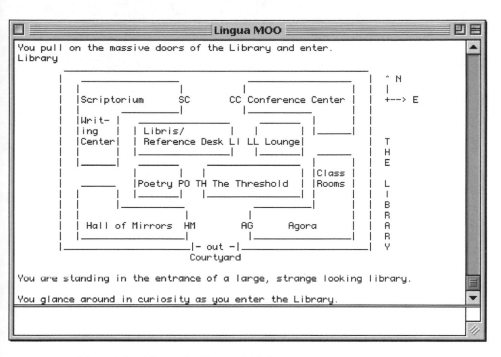

FIGURE 6.4   Map of the Library in Lingua MOO

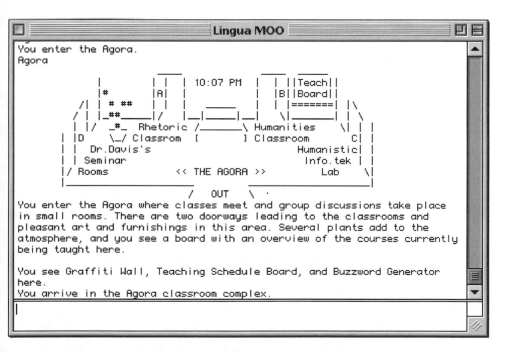

FIGURE 6.5   Map of the Lingua MOO Classroom Complex

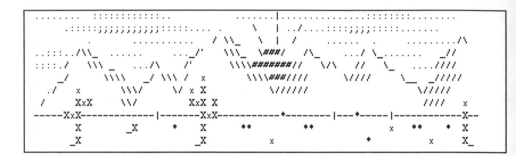

FIGURE 6.6 ASCII Graphic of Sunrise over Ghost Ranch, New Mexico

If you want to use ASCII graphics or maps,[1] be sure not to include them in the textual description of the object; instead put them in a special *property* called *drawing* that can be found on every object (please see Chapter 7 for more on properties). We strongly recommend that you prepare your map or graphic in your favorite text editor where you can edit it easily and then transfer it to the MOO using the text editor's *enter* function as described in Chapter 5. To open the text editor and start editing an object's drawing property, type *@notedit object.drawing.* For example, if you want to create a map of your room you should type *@notedit here.drawing.*

If you do decide to make a map of your room, you can put the name of the exits from your room on the map as shown in Figures 6.4 and 6.5 so that visitors can see them easily.

There are several reasons why we recommend that you do not include ASCII graphics with the descriptions of objects. First of all, people who are using speech recognition and text syntheticization software should be able to turn graphics off and on using the *@ascii off* and *@ascii on* commands if they wish. Second, if you do place the ASCII graphic together with the description of the object, it will come out all skewed and incomprehensible when viewed from the Web.

If you are using enCore Xpress you can easily add and edit ASCII art and maps using the Xpress Object Editor. Simply put them in the area designated for ASCII drawings.

Adding Multimedia Content to Your Objects

Because of the tight World Wide Web integration offered by enCore-based MOOs, using the Xpress system you can easily add multimedia features such as icons, images, sound, animations, or even interactive Java applets to your rooms and objects. Adding such features is not complicated, but it does involve a basic understanding of how a Web page is composed. For a thorough introduction to Web composition and how to create Web sites, we refer you to Victor Vitanza's[2] *Writing for the World Wide Web.* In this chapter, however, suffice it to say that a Web page is composed of two entities: text and other *elements.* As noted above, the text, which includes the HTML code that is used to produce the Web layout, is automatically generated for you by the MOO, so you don't have to worry about that. The other elements, however, such as images, sound files, Shockwave animations, Java applets, and more, are not part of the Web page itself (not in the way that illustrations are integrated parts of word processing documents). Instead, these elements are data files that exist separately somewhere on the Web, and we *embed* them in our Web pages by linking to them.

(i)

URL stands for Uniform Resource Locator and is a unique pointer to a file accessible via the Internet. In the hypertext transfer protocol (http), which is used to transfer files over the World Wide Web, the first part of a URL refers to where in the world a computer is located. The second part refers to where on the computer pointed to by the first part of the URL the file we want is located. For example, the following URL http://lingua.utdallas.edu/jan/index.html points to a file called *index.html* which is located in a folder called *jan,* on a machine named *lingua,* which is located at University of Texas at Dallas in the United States.

The enCore Xpress system allows you to link to elements such as those mentioned by connecting their URLs to the objects you want. The general command for this purpose is *connect URL to object.* In the following discussion, we'll give some examples that illustrate how you can use the connect command to add multimedia content to your MOO objects. Let's say you have a photo of yourself on the Web somewhere that you want to attach to your MOO character so others will see it when they look at you. This is easily done by typing *connect http://server.site.domain/directory/photo.jpg to me.* Note that the URL given here is generic and should be replaced with the real URL pointing to your photo file. Further, you may have an object called Painting in your room that is described as your favorite painting by Henri Matisse. If you happen to find a picture of this painting on the Web, you can easily connect it to your painting object with the command *connect URL to painting*. Whenever somebody looks at your painting, they will now be able to see the picture along with your description of it.

Instead of using the *connect* command, you can also enter the URL for the external multimedia content in the field designated for URLs in the Xpress Object Editor.

To further illustrate how you may use enCore Xpress to add multimedia content to the MOO, consider the following examples. Say you want to be able to listen to your favorite radio station or watch your favorite TV programs in the MOO. Impossible you say? Well, not if that radio or TV station broadcasts via Real Audio or Real Video, for example, and you have the correct plug-in installed in your Web browser. Create an object called, for example, TV. Locate the URL that delivers the live audio or video stream and connect the URL to the TV object. Look at the TV and *voila!* You and others can listen to radio or watch TV while MOOing. You may also connect Java applets to your MOO creations. Because Java is a complete programming language, there are virtually no limits to the kind of interactivity that can be integrated into the MOO. Consider, for example, a biology class where you can dissect virtual frogs and fish in the MOO classroom!

Building and creating objects on the MOO can be time-consuming, but fun and artistic. You also have the satisfaction of knowing that you are contributing to the MOO community with your creations. One of the most distinguishing features of MOOs is that they are an ever-changing, dynamic evolution and convolution of people, language, computer code, and time. MOOs are constantly works-in-progress as users add and revise the space— and all in writing! Each layer of the MOO (the public space, the players' rooms, the interMOO channels of communication, the real-time classes and events, the interactive objects) makes it a much more palpable, lived space. In the next chapter, you will tackle the innermost workings of a MOO by learning to write the programs that make the MOO function. You'll be surprised to know that programming is writing! It has its own code and method of communication, even if that language is transmitted between databases by machines. Just as you need to be precise in formal writing, using correct syntax and grammar, programming requires equal attention to precision. You can become part of the revolution in which writing technologies are encompassing modes of writing previously confined to the computer sciences, but now are making their way into the heart of the humanities.

NOTES

1. For a good source of free ASCII graphic art, check out this Web site in Norway:

   http://wigwam.askoyv.no/Ascii/

2. For information on Vitanza's *Writing for the World Wide Web* and his *CyberReader,* both from Allyn & Bacon, go to:

   http://www.abacon.com/vitanza/

CLASS DISCUSSION

1. Discuss MOO architecture and how you use language and text as building blocks when you dig and create objects in the MOO. In what ways does this affect the MOO experience? How does it relate to "reading" in general?

2. Get into groups (either in RL or online) and make a list of your ideas for the next generation of MOO architecture. Don't think in terms of buildings, rooms, halls, doors, and so on. What kind of spaces are possible in MOOs? How would you describe them? How would they alter the way we communicate on the MOO, or would they? How would you build them? What new metaphors can you create with which to build a new archi-texture? Stretch your imagination!

3. Break into groups on the MOO and have your teacher record each group discussion. The discussion topic is "recording discussions" and you should think in terms of sketching lists of pros and cons about having your group discussions recorded. As a follow-up assignment, analyze the log of your discussion to get an overview of the various opinions and make notes about how discussion actually occurs. Who speaks the most? Who the least? Why? What could be done to encourage discussion? What are the reactions of students in your class to "playful" parts of the conversation? How should these logs be archived? Or should they? Would you consider such logs as "publications"?

EXERCISES

1. Build a room or set of rooms and describe them as true real-life rooms or as hypertexts. From what you learned about how to describe your room, see what you can do with using a "room" to contain in its description a text or essay or poem. Experiment, in other words, with various ways to "use" the MOO room. Keep good notes in your MOO notebook as you go, and don't forget to recycle objects or rooms you decide not to keep.

2. Create a set of *$notes* with information about your room(s)/text(s) and drop them in your room as objects for visitors to your room to read. Using the help information about *$notes,* practice encrypting a note and decrypting it.

3. Following your class discussion about recording such discussions, create your own recorder and use it to record a discussion about how logs can be used effectively. Make notes about how the recorder works and which logs are stored in it

once you finish recording. Finally, e-mail the log to yourself using the *mailme* command and recycle the log.

4. Using the ideas your class discussed about new MOO architectural metaphors, plan a small matrix of "rooms" or spaces (depending on your new metaphor); using your MOO notebook, outline a plan for implementing your project. Be creative! Go wild!

5. Check out the ASCII graphics Web site listed above in Notes and practice creating your own ASCII graphic for your room using a word file offline for drafting the graphic. Experiment with font and size, though Courier 9 or 10 usually pastes well into the MOO. Remember that you need to paste such graphics in the *.drawing* property of your room. Use your MOO notebook to sketch possible drawings.

REFERENCES

Vitanza, Victor J. *Writing for the World Wide Web*. Boston: Allyn & Bacon, 1998.

CHAPTER

7 Object-Oriented Programming in the MOO

In addition to the tools and features we have discussed in the previous chapters, the MOO is also a powerful *object-oriented programming* environment. Object-oriented programming (OOP) is the dominant way that computer programs are written today. Whether you just want to experiment by writing a few simple MOO programs, or if you want to use this experience as a springboard for learning how to program in other languages (such as Java or C++), the MOO makes learning programming fun and easy.

In this chapter we will introduce you to object-oriented design and programming in the MOO. We start out by discussing some of the basic principles of object-oriented programming and how you use them to design your own programs. We also talk briefly about the basic building blocks in the MOO programming language, and how you use them to write your own programs. We will take you step-by-step through a concrete example of how a MOO program is written, so we recommend that you stay logged on to the MOO while working on the examples and exercises in this chapter. No book can teach you how to program unless you also practice what you learn by trying it out on the computer. We can teach you the theory, but in the end, only through practice and patience will you become a MOO programmer.

Becoming a Programmer: The First Steps

In order to program in the MOO, your character needs to be a programmer. Becoming a programmer is much like becoming a builder as we talked about in the previous chapter. You need to talk to your teacher or one of the MOO administrators and ask if you can get what we on the MOO call a "programmer bit." When talking to a MOO administrator, it is a good idea to explain why you want to become a programmer in the MOO, and what you plan to program and create. Of course, you won't know in advance all the things you may want to program down the road, but from a MOO administrator's point of view, it is always good to have an idea of what a new programmer wants to do before making someone a programmer.

Becoming a MOO programmer is a privilege that will empower you with tools to create much more elaborate and interactive things than you could as a builder. With the MOO programming language you can program almost anything you want. Along with this privilege, however, goes a responsibility. Every programmer can make a mistake, and such mistakes often prove to be valuable lessons. However, writing malicious programs with the intent to invade other people's privacy, or, even worse, compromise the security or operation of the whole MOO is not only unethical, but we can guarantee that it will have severe repercussions that you just don't want to deal with. So be cool, have fun, and enjoy your MOO programming experience.

Object-Oriented Concepts

One way to think about object-oriented systems is to imagine a box of Lego bricks. The Lego bricks come in a variety of shapes, colors, and sizes, and you can use them to create almost anything imaginable. By snapping together in-dividual Lego bricks you can form bigger pieces that can themselves be com-bined into even bigger and more elaborate creations. Just as the Lego brick is the nuclear entity of Lego constructions, the object is the nuclear entity of object-oriented systems. In the MOO, everything is an object—from the sim-plest note to the most complex room, they are all objects.

(!)

Like Lego bricks, objects can be combined to form more elaborate creations, and in the MOO objects typically build on one another to form more refined *classes of objects*. A *class* is, by definition, a group of objects that are interre-lated through a mechanism called *inheritance*. Figure 7.1 shows the basic class structure in the MOO. Please note that the figure only shows some of the classes commonly found in MOOs, and some of them may only be avail-able in MOOs based on the High Wired enCore educational MOO database.

As Figure 7.1 illustrates, all objects in the MOO are based on the *Root Class*. This class defines certain common characteristics for all objects in the MOO. Based on the root class, we find the following *subclasses:* $thing, $room, and $player. These classes are *refined instances of the root class*, each tailored toward a different abstract concept, namely that of a thing, a room, and a player. *Abstraction* is a key concept in object-oriented thinking, and, as Figure 7.1 illustrates, object-oriented systems such as the MOO are always

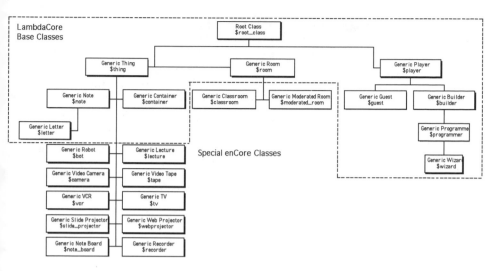

FIGURE 7.1   MOO Class Hierarchy

built up from the most abstract objects toward more and more refined and concrete objects. For example, under the class $thing, we find the subclasses $note and $container, which are more concrete things, and under the class $note, we find the subclass $letter.

We mentioned previously that in the MOO objects are grouped together into classes through a mechanism called *inheritance*. What this actually means is that each object inherits layers of characteristics from its *parent classes* (also known as *super classes*), and adds a new layer of characteristics of its own. Figure 7.2 illustrates how the inheritance mechanism works to form a class out of several individual objects.

(i)

Kristen Nygaard and Ole-Johan Dahl of the Norwegian Computing Center in Oslo, Norway first developed the principles of object-oriented programming (OOP) back in the mid-1960s. Their programming language, Simula 67, which was developed as a general purpose programming language geared toward discrete event simulations, became the first computer programming language to sport such common object-oriented concepts as abstraction, objects and classes, inheritance, and polymorphism. In the 1970s, the concepts of OOP were discovered by Alan Kay of Xerox PARC and formed the basis for his programming language called *Smalltalk*. With the adoption of object-oriented principles in Bjarne Stroustrup's highly popular C++ language in the 1980s, and, most recently, with the Java programming language from Sun

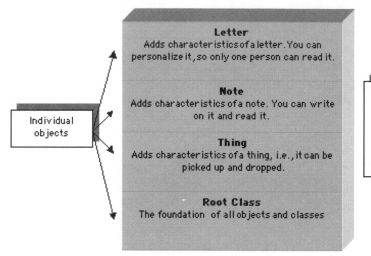

FIGURE 7.2   Construction of Classes through Inheritance

Microsystems in the 1990s, OOP has, in effect, become the dominant paradigm in computer science today.[1] The MOO programming language was originally conceived by Stephen White around 1990, but it was Pavel Curtis, a research scientist of Xerox PARC, who did the main development and documentation of the language.

The Anatomy of the Object: Verbs and Properties

A closer look at the MOO object reveals that it is composed of two elements: *verbs* and *properties*, illustrated in Figure 7.3.[2]

A verb is the same as a program, that is, an algorithm, or recipe, that contains a detailed step-by-step description for how the computer is to solve a given problem. Verbs always reside on objects and typically define ways in which users can interact with the object on which they reside. For example, when you read a note in the MOO by typing *read note*, you are actually *running a verb* named *read* that is defined on the object called *note*. This verb contains instructions that tell the computer to display the text that is written on the note object. Verbs can also perform other tasks that don't involve user interaction, such as backing up the whole MOO at given intervals.

A property, on the other hand, is a slot on the object that typically contains data about the object such as its name, description, location, owner, and so forth. Unlike verbs, properties cannot perform any operations; they are

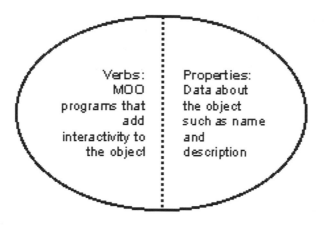

FIGURE 7.3   **The Anatomy of the MOO Object**

merely containers for data, either about the object on which they reside, or, in some cases, about some other object or structure in the MOO.

When we talked about inherited characteristics above, what we really referred to were the verbs and properties we have just discussed. In the remainder of this chapter we will take you through a complete MOO programming example and show you how the principles of object-oriented programming really work, and how you can use them to construct your own interactive objects with verbs and properties.

Object-Oriented Design

The programming example that we are going to show you in this chapter is how to create and program a generic drink that can, perhaps, be used to create a bottle of soda that you can enjoy while hanging out with your friends in the MOO. Before we delve into the actual programming of this object, however, we need to plan how we are going to implement a virtual representation of a drink in the text-based MOO world.

In object-oriented environments, the first step in this planning process is called *abstraction*. Recall that in the MOO objects build on one another to form classes, from the most general and abstract to the more refined and concrete. Thus, the first thing we should do is to determine what kind of abstract object a drink is, and on which, if any, preexisting class in the MOO we should base our new creation. By looking at the overview of preexisting classes in the MOO (Figure 7.1), we can easily determine that a drink is a thing, and it should be based on the class thing, also called *generic thing*. We can now create our new object with the following command: (Please note that in all our examples below [except for pseudocode], the commands that you should type are boldfaced and the MOO's response is printed in lightface directly following the command. If no MOO response is in our example, the text will be in lightface. Some of the object numbers in these examples will be different for you. Finally, when typing a line, as our examples will show, assume that you should hit the enter or return key to complete the action.)

```
@create $thing named Generic Drink, drink
You now have Generic Drink (aka drink) with object number
#1663 and parent generic thing (#5).
```

This command creates a new object that is a subclass of *$thing* with the name *Generic Drink* and alias *drink* (Figure 7.4). Because we made our new object a subclass of the Generic Thing, we can already start to interact with it. We can, for example, drop it on the floor and pick it up again. In object-oriented terms, we say that the new Generic Drink inherits these characteristics from its super class, Generic Thing.

The next step in the abstraction process is to strip away as many of the characteristics specific to a drink as we can until only its most abstract and general features remain. At this point we are not interested in what kind of drink it is we are creating, what it tastes like, or what color it is. Instead, we are interested in the abstract features that distinguish a drink from other objects. One such feature is that you can drink it. If we really put our mind to it, we could undoubtedly come up with a number of other distinguishing features for a drink, but for now this is the only feature we want to consider. So how are we going to drink something in a virtual reality that is nothing but text? Well, here is where your creativity and programming come in. What we must do is define and program a verb called *drink* on the Generic Drink object.

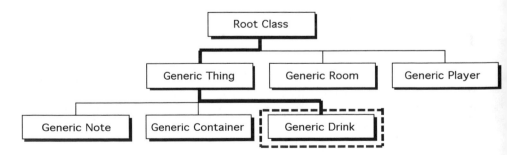

FIGURE 7.4   **Generic Drink Class Hierarchy**

Creating a Test Object

Generic objects should only be used to put verbs and properties on; they should never be used to interact with. For this purpose we create a subclass that we can use to experiment with.

```
@create "Generic Drink" named soda
@describe soda as "You see a bottle of soda."
```

The new object named soda is a subclass of drink, and will inherit any verbs and properties that we decide to define on the generic drink.

Before you start to actually program the *drink* verb, it is often helpful to describe, in very general terms, what the verb is supposed to do. This method is called *pseudocode*, and it is not something a computer is supposed to understand. Instead, it is a way for you to understand and plan the structure of your verb. The pseudocode for our *drink* verb might look something like the following:

```
When someone types drink soda:
The drink verb tells that person that "You drink soda."
It tells other people who are present that "Someone drinks
soda."

End of verb
```

After reviewing our pseudocode we realize that we also want a place to store information about how a specific drink tastes. For this purpose we need a property to hold this information.

We are now through with the preliminary design process, and we can conclude that we need:

- One verb called *drink* on the object Generic Drink, and
- One property on the same object that we call *taste*

Defining Verbs: Arguments

Creating a verb is done in two steps. First you need to define the verb on an object, and then you need to program the verb itself. The process of defining a new verb can be a little confusing, so we are going to explain it in some detail here.

Because the MOO is a text-based, command line oriented system, verbs are usually invoked when someone types a command that executes them, as, for example, when someone types the command *read book* to read a book they come across. In order to execute the correct verb, the MOO needs to know on what object it is defined (the direct object) and whether or not a preposition or an indirect object is allowed as part of the command syntax (for example, in the command *put book in shelf*). All this information must be provided when we create the verb, so let us now look at how verbs are defined and arguments are specified.

```
@verb object:verb direct_object preposition indirect_object
```

This is the general syntax of the *@verb* command. It tells the MOO to define a new verb on the specified object with the specified arguments, that is, direct object, preposition, and indirect object.

Please note that a colon is always used to separate objects and verbs. Also, verb names as well as property names cannot contain any spaces. When defining a new verb, the three variables in Table 7.1 are used to represent the arguments:

TABLE 7.1   Verb Argument Variables

Variable	Explanation
This	Refers to the object on which the verb is defined
Any	Refers to any object, meaning that the MOO will accept any value that is placed here
None	Indicates no verb argument

The verb arguments can be composed of any of these three variables, plus a legal preposition as shown in Table 7.2.

When defining a verb and its arguments, it is often helpful to think about it in terms of what you want to type in order to execute the verb. In our example we want the command syntax to read:

```
Drink name_of_drink
```

Please note that English articles (*i.e., the, a,* and *an*) are not generally used in MOO commands. Because the direct object in this case is the Generic Drink, we use the variable *this* for the direct object; because we don't want

**TABLE 7.2   Overview of Legal Verb Arguments
and Prepositions in the MOO**

Direct Object	Preposition	Indirect Object
This	Any	This
Any	None	Any
None		None
	with/using	
	at/to	
	in front of	
	in/inside/into	
	on top of/on/onto/upon	
	out of/from inside/from	
	over	
	through	
	under/underneath/	
	beneath	
	behind	
	beside	
	for/about	
	is	
	as	
	off/off of	

any prepositions or indirect objects, we use the variable *none* to represent both of these arguments. In order to define the new verb *drink* on the Generic Drink object with these arguments, we type:

```
@verb "Generic Drink":drink this none none
Verb added (0).
```

Dealing with verb arguments is probably going to be quite confusing at first, but don't forget, always think about them in terms of how you want your command syntax to read. To illustrate this, let us consider another example. Imagine that you have created an object called *snow,* and now you want to define a verb called *throw* on the snow object so you and your friends can have a virtual snowball fight. If you just want people to be able to grab some snow and throw it somewhere, the command would be *throw snow,* and the verb arguments would read *this none none,* as in the drink example. If, on the other hand, you want something more fun and devious, namely, to allow people to throw snow at one another, the command should be something like *throw snow at person,* and the verb arguments should read *this at any.* In this last example we are using the preposition *at* and the variable *any* so that people can throw their snowball at whomever they wish.

Defining Properties

Now that we have defined our *drink* verb, we should also define the message property we want. Although working with properties is easier and less confusing than dealing with verb arguments, there is one important thing to consider. Earlier we said that properties are data slots, and, for this reason, we need to make sure that they have the correct format to hold the type of data we want to put in them. In other words, when we define a property we must first decide what *data type* it should hold. Properties and other variables in the MOO can hold five different types of data: object numbers, integers, decimal numbers, characters strings, and lists that can be composed of any of these data types (see Table 7.3).

If you want to create a property that can store numbers with which you can perform mathematical operations such as addition, subtraction, multiplication, or division, then your property must be given the data type integer or

TABLE 7.3   **MOO Data Types**

Data type	Explanation	Init value	Example
Object Number	A reference to an object in the MOO. The hash mark (#) must always be included.	An object number	#100
Integer	A positive or negative number	A number, default is 0	1
Floating Point Number	A decimal number	A decimal number	1.2
String	A set of characters enclosed in double quote marks	An empty string consisting only of two double quote marks, ""	"This is a string"
List	An array that can contain all the data types above. Curly brackets are used to denote a list, and commas are used to separate elements in the list.	An empty list consisting only of two curly brackets, {}	{"This", "is", "a", "list", "of", "strings"}

floating point. If, on the other hand, you want to put alphanumeric characters, that is, text, in the property, it must be declared as a string or a list of strings.

The general format of the command we use to create properties looks like

```
@property object.property_name data_type init_value
```

Just as when we are creating new verbs, we first need to specify on what object we want to define the new property and what name we want to give it. In addition, we must also decide what data type the property should hold and whether or not we want to give it an initial value, that is, put something in the property when we first create it.

Note that a period is always used to separate object names and property names.

Making sure that we select the correct data type for the properties we create is very important. Let's say we have two variables called A and B. Both of these variables contain the number 1. If we perform the following mathematical operation, the answer will be:

```
A + B = 2
1 + 1 = 2
```

Now, let's say we change the data type of the two variables to string and put the character "1" in each of them. To the human eye this may not look much different than the example above, but see what happens when we perform the same operation:

```
A + B = 11
"1" + "1" = "11"
```

In the first case, when we add two numbers (integers) we get the expected answer, namely 2. In the second case, however, we are not adding numbers at all, instead, we are adding the character "1" to another character "1," and the result is a concatenation of the two that results in the string "11."

In our Generic Drink program we want to store textual information about what our drink tastes like in a property, and thus it needs to be of the data-type string.

```
@property "Generic Drink".messages ""
Property added with value "".
```

So far, we have

- Created a *new object* called Generic Drink with super class Generic Thing;
- Created a test object called soda with super class Generic Drink;
- Created a *new verb* called drink with the *arguments this none none* on the object Generic Drink;
- Created a *new property* called taste *of the data type string* on the object Generic Drink.

The Building Blocks of the MOO Language: Expressions, Statements, and Operators

The process of writing a MOO verb or any other computer program for that matter is called *coding*. Unlike the pseudocode that we wrote earlier, a verb must be written in a code that the MOO can interpret. This code is the MOO programming language. It goes without saying that we cannot possibly teach you everything about the MOO language in this chapter, but we will show you some of its main constructs and features and how to use them to construct your own programs.

Like any kind of writing, the MOO language has a grammar, or syntax. While human readers are quite forgiving when it comes to bad grammar, the MOO is not. In your class papers, you can probably get away with using a colon when you are supposed to use a semicolon, or a period instead of a comma; your reader will still understand what you mean. If, however, you make the same mistake in a verb, the MOO will not understand what you mean, and it will flat out refuse to accept your program. In order for the MOO to understand the code that you write, it must therefore adhere to a very strict syntax, which is defined in the MOO language. At the simplest level, this syntax consists of *expressions* and *statements* separated by semicolons. It is a combination of statements and expressions that make up the body of your verb program.

Expressions

Expressions are bits of code that generate values. They are the most basic elements in MOO code. An example of an expression is:

```
2 + 2 = 4
```

The expression above generates the value 4. In most cases the programmer wants to use *variables* instead of absolute values in expressions. A variable is a temporary place to store values that the MOO program uses. Like properties that we have discussed above, variables have names and they must be assigned to specific data types (see Table 7.3). However, unlike properties that are, in principle, accessible from any verb in the MOO, variables are always local to the verb in which they are declared. Furthermore, variables are only temporary; that is, they disappear when the verb that declared them stops running. Properties on the other hand are permanent, they retain their assigned value until it is either changed or the property is removed. For these reasons, we can refer to variables that appear inside MOO verbs as *local variables,* whereas properties defined on objects can be referred to as *global variables.*

```
Number1 = 2;
Number2 = 2;
Answer = number1 + number2;
```

This is an example of how variables are used to represent values in MOO code. First we create a variable called number1 and initialize it with the value 2. Because the initialization value we are using is an integer, the new variable is automatically of the data type integer. Next we create a second variable called number2, also initialized to the integer 2. In the last line we instruct the MOO to take the contents of the variable called number1 and add it to the contents of the variable called number2, and then place the result in a variable called *answer.* In addition to variables that we declare in the programs we write, there are also a number of special *reserved variables* that the MOO uses to hold certain values that are often referred to. For instance, the special variable *player* always refers to the person who types the command that invokes the verb in which the variable occurs. [The special variable *this* always refers to the object on which a verb is defined.] For a complete list of these special variables, see Table 7.4.

Statements

Statements in the MOO language are constructs that perform structural, nonvalue-generating operations. We consider them one step up from expressions, and the two types we are going to consider here are:

- Selection statements
- Iteration statements

Statements provide structure to your verbs and allow you to create really advanced programs, so we'll cover the ones you will probably be using the most.

TABLE 7.4   **Reserved Variables in the MOO Language.**

Reserved Variables	Explanation
player	an object, the player who typed the command
this	an object, the object on which this verb was found
caller	an object, the same as 'player'
verb	a string, the first word of the command
argstr	a string, everything after the first word of the command
args	a list of strings, the words in 'argstr'
dobjstr	a string, the direct object string found during parsing
dobj	an object, the direct object value found during matching
prepstr	a string, the prepositional phrase found during parsing
iobjstr	a string, the indirect object string
iobj	an object, the indirect object value

Source: MOO Programmers Manual

The **If-Statement.**   The *if-statement* is designed to let you select what action your program should take based on the result of some condition. In the following example, the program is told to check whether the sun is shining. If it is true that it is shining, you should go to the beach. In this case the condition is whether the sun is shining or not. In a real MOO program, the condition will usually be an evaluation of some expression.

```
if (sunny weather)
   Go to the beach
endif
```

Sometimes you may want your program to do one thing if a condition is true and something else if it's not. For this purpose you have the *else* construct.

```
if (sunny weather)
   Go to the beach
else
   Study for class
endif
```

Other times you may need to test for several conditions to determine what action your program should take. The *elseif* construct is what you use in these cases.

```
if (sunny weather)
   Go to the beach
elseif (class tomorrow)
   Study for class
else
   Go to the movies
endif
```

You can also test for conditions within conditions in a nested fashion.

```
if (sunny weather)
   Go to the beach
elseif (class tomorrow)
   if (class on the MOO)
      read MOOniversity
   else
      Study assigned readings
   endif
else
   Go to the movies
endif
```

If-statements must always be closed with an *endif* construct. Each *if*-statement must have its own *endif*.

The For-Statement.   Sometimes you want your program to perform certain expressions and/or statements a number of times. For these situations, the MOO provides the *for-statement*. This is an iteration statement that will run in a loop until a certain condition is met.

```
For (First to last chocolate in box)
   Eat one chocolate
Endfor
```

```
For ( 1 to 3)
   Shout "Hip, hip hurray"
Endfor
```

In the first of these two examples we tell the computer to run in a loop until we have eaten all the chocolates in the box. The *for*-statement is very useful when we want to cycle through a set of data when we know in advance its size. Examples of such data sets are all the numbers between one and, say, ten, or the contents of a list property in the MOO. *For*-statements must always be closed with an *endfor* construct.

The **While-*Statement.***   The *while-statement* is also an iteration statement, but unlike the *for*-statement, we use this statement when we don't know in advance how many times our program should loop through a set of expressions and/or statements.

```
While (the sun is shining)
   Hang out at the beach and get a tan
endwhile
```

In this example we cannot know in advance how long the sun is going to shine, but we do know we want to stay at the beach until it starts to rain or the sun goes down. Therefore, we tell the MOO to keep checking whether the sun is still shining and not send us home until this condition is no longer true. Like the other statements we have talked about, the *while*-statement must also be closed using the *endwhile* construct.

Operators

We use *operators* to manipulate expressions and statements. In the example of variables above we used the operator, +, to add two variables, and the assignment operator, =, to assign values. Table 7.5 provides an overview of some of the operators available in the MOO.

Although the MOO language was designed to be simple and easy to learn for beginners, it is remarkably sophisticated, and once you learn how to use it, you can program really advanced programs in the MOO. In this section we have only talked about a few of the many features of the MOO language. If you want to know more about it and its many features, we encourage you to take a look at *The MOO Programmers Manual.* (You will find a reference to it at the end of this chapter.)

Writing Your First Verb

Although some of the things we have talked about thus far in this chapter may seem utterly confusing at this point, do not despair. Remember what we said at the beginning: The only way to learn programming is to practice writing programs and try them out on the MOO. That is precisely what we are going to do now.

Let us first review the pseudocode we wrote for our little *drink* verb.

```
When someone types drink soda:
The drink verb tells that person that "You drink soda."
It tells other people who are present that "Someone drinks
soda."
End of verb
```

TABLE 7.5   Overview of Some Frequently Used MOO Operators

Arithmetic Operators

Operator	Name	Example
+	Addition	2 + 2 = 4 "Hi" + " There" = "Hi There"
–	Subtraction	3 – 1 = 2
*	Multiplication	5 * 3 = 15
/	Division	10 / 2 = 5

Assignment Operator

=	Assign	2 + 2 = 4

Value Comparison Operators

==	Equals	3 == 4 = FALSE
		5 == 5 = TRUE
!=	Not equals	2 != 5 = TRUE
<	Less than	4 < 3 = FALSE
>	Greater than	7 > 5 = TRUE
<=	Less or equal to	7 <= 5 = FALSE
		5 <= 5 = TRUE
>=	Greater or equal to	10 > 7 = TRUE

Boolean Operators

&&	And	Compares two expressions, both must return TRUE in order for the result to be TRUE
| |	Or	Compares two expressions, at least one must return TRUE in order for the result to be TRUE
!	Not	Negation. Turns TRUE to FALSE and FALSE to TRUE.

Based on the pseudocode we can determine that we need a way to display the text we want, first to the person who actually drinks our soda, and then to anyone else who happens to be present. Luckily, routines for these purposes have already been programmed in the MOO, so we can simply use them in our verb. When we use a verb inside another verb, we say that we *call the verb*. The first verb we need to call is named *tell*, and it is defined on the Generic Player. The second verb is called *announce*, and it is defined on the Generic Room. Here is how our *drink* verb looks in MOO code:

```
Player:tell("You drink", this.name);
Player.location:announce(player.name, " drinks",
this.name);
```

Let's take a moment to explain what actually goes on in the two lines of code. First, the *drink* verb on soda, which is actually inherited from Generic Drink, calls the verb *tell*, which is defined on Generic Player. Recall that *player* is a special variable that always refers to the person who issues a command. Because this person's character in the MOO belongs to the class generic player, the *tell* verb will direct its output to this person. The second part of the first sentence consists of what we call the *argument* that is being passed to $player:tell. This argument is in fact a string that is made up of the words, *You drink*, plus a property called *this.name*. When we talked about properties and variables earlier, we said that *this* is a special variable used by the MOO in reference to the object on which the calling verb, *drink*, is defined. In our case, that object is Generic Drink; but soda inherits the verb, so the content of the property referred to by *this.name* is actually the name *soda*.

In line two we call another verb named *announce*. This verb is located on the object referred to by a property called *player.location*. Because we already know that *player* always refers to a person, and that the property *location*, which is defined on $player, usually refers to the room the player is in, we can determine that *player.location* refers to a room. In other words, we are calling a verb named *announce* that is defined on the Generic room but inherited by the room that the player is presently in. The argument that we are passing to this verb is essentially the same as in the first line, with the exception that this time we also include a reference (player.name) to the player who drank our soda, so that folks know who did it.

That was a mouthful, wasn't it? Let's try to program the verb now and see what happens.

Programming Verbs

In the MOO there are essentially two ways to program verbs. The first is by using the MOO's *verb editor*, and the second is by using a special command called *@program*. The verb editor works in exactly the same way as the mail and note editors, which we discussed in detail in Chapter 5, so we won't go into detail about it here. Instead, we'll explain how to use the *@program* command to program your MOO verbs.

Using the *@program* command is similar to the various paste functions that we have already discussed (see Chapter 5), in the sense that you prepare your code offline in your favorite text editor and then paste it into the MOO with *@program*. This approach has a number of benefits over using the MOO's verb editor. First of all it makes it much easier to edit your code and fix errors; secondly, you'll always have a backup of your code in a file on your computer in case the MOO should crash and your work is lost. The syntax for the *@program* command is:

```
@program object:verb
```

Just as in the case of *@verb*, object refers to the object on which the verb we want to program is defined, and verb specifies the name of the verb we wish to program. Thus, in our example we should type:

```
@program "Generic Drink":drink
Player:tell("You drink ", this.name);
Player.location:announce(player.name, " drinks ", this.name);
```

Now paste or type in the lines of code that we wrote above. Finish with a period on a line by itself, press the enter or return key, and our verb should *compile*. To compile a verb or a program means to translate it into a form that the computer can understand.

Now let's try out our new drink by typing:

```
Drink soda
```

Congratulations, you have just programmed your first MOO verb! Go and grab a real soft drink, you deserve it :-).

Assigning Values to Properties

Let us now try expanding our verb a little to make it more interesting. So far our drink doesn't taste like anything, so let's fix that next. If you recall, we have already defined a property on the Generic Drink called *taste*, and this is where we want to put a textual description of what our drink tastes like. If we place this description on the object Generic Drink, however, all sub-classes will inherit it, so instead we want to put it on the soda object. The command that is used to assign values to properties is called *@set*, and here is how it generally looks:

```
@set object.property to value
```

As usual, we must specify what object and which property on that object we want to change, so in order to describe what our soda tastes like, we type:

```
@set soda.taste to "cold and refreshing"
```

Now that we have specified a taste, let us reprogram our *drink* verb to include it. To do this, you can simply type or paste the lines below into your MOO window.

```
@program "Generic Drink":drink
Player:tell("You take a swig of ", this.taste, " ", this.name);
```

```
Player.location:announce(player.name, " takes a big swig of ",
this.taste, " ", this.name);
```

Getting Braver: A More Complex Example

After having played around with your drink for a while you have probably noticed that it never gets empty. Although this may be a fascinating concept, it is hardly very realistic, so let's see if we can't program some realism into our *drink* verb. The first thing we want to do is outline the new structure of the verb using pseudocode.

```
When someone types drink soda:
Check to see if the drink is empty
If the drink is empty
     Tell player that the drink is empty and that he or she
     needs to refill it.
If the drink is not empty
     Tell player that you drink soda
     Tell other people that player drinks soda.
Make a note of how many swigs are left in the drink.
End of verb
```

Based on this outline we can see that in this new version of the *drink* verb we'll need to use *the selection statement If* in order to determine what the verb should display. In addition, we need some sort of counter that can keep track of how many more times someone can drink our soda before it's empty. This counter cannot be a local variable because then it will disappear as soon as the execution of the *drink* verb is over. It must therefore be a global variable, in other words, a property. We want the drink to be full the first time someone finds it, and to accomplish this we need to give the new variable an initial value that is greater than 0.

```
@property "Generic Drink".swigs 5
```

Next we reprogram our verb. The result will look something like:

```
@program "Generic Drink":drink
swigs_left = this.swigs;
if (swigs_left == 0)
    player:tell("The ", this.name, " is empty. You need to
    refill it.");
else
    Player:tell("You take a swig of ", this.taste, " ",
    this.name);
```

```
Player.location:announce(player.name, " takes a big swig
of ", this.taste, " ", this.name);
Swigs_left = swigs_left - 1;
This.swigs = swigs_left;
endif
```

In this program we are demonstrating a number of things that we have talked about in this chapter. Let's therefore explain it line by line.

In the first line we create a local variable called *swigs_left,* and assign it the value of the property swigs on the object. Next, we use an *If-*statement to check if the variable *swigs_left* is equal to 0. Note that we use the operator == here, not =, which is the assignment operator. It's very easy to confuse these two, so keep in mind that they are different. If it turns out that the variable *swigs_left* is indeed equal to 0, the program tells the player this. Then, it jumps to the last *endif* and stops running. On the other hand, if *swigs_left* is not equal to 0, which means we can still drink more, the program informs the player and others who happen to be present that the player drinks something. Now that someone has reduced the contents in our drink, we need to record that, so we reduce the value of the local property *swigs_left* by 1, and, finally, we update the property swigs on the object to reflect this reduction in contents. The program then exits and stops running.

After you have taken five swigs of your soda you will notice that you cannot drink any more until you refill it. To accomplish this, we need to program another verb on the Generic Drink that we call refill. Below are the commands and code needed to implement this verb.

```
@verb "Generic Drink":refill this none none
@program "Generic Drink":refill
if (this.swigs == 0)
    this.swigs = 5;
    player:tell("You refill the ", this.name);
    player.location:announce(player.name, " refills the ",
    this.name);
else
    player:tell("The ", this.name, " is not empty yet.");
endif
```

Based on your new generic drink you can now experiment with making various kinds of drinks, such as juice, wine, beer, and so forth. All you need to do is create new objects using your Generic Drink as the super class, describing them and giving them individual tastes. When you have created a few new drinks you can perhaps open a cafe and invite your friends over for a virtual party.

Programming with the enCore Xpress Verb Editor

If you are using the enCore Xpress system, programming in the MOO will be greatly simplified. This system has an editor that provides both an overview and easy access to verbs and their properties. A screenshot of how this Xpress editor looks is shown in Figure 7.5. In addition to the simplified MOO programming through the graphical Verb Editor interface, Xpress users will also benefit from the easy-to-use Xpress Property Editor, shown in Figure 7.6.

From the Programmer's Toolbox

In addition to the commands we have discussed so far, as a programmer you'll have a number of other useful commands available to you. We cannot possibly cover them all in this chapter, but most of them are well docu-

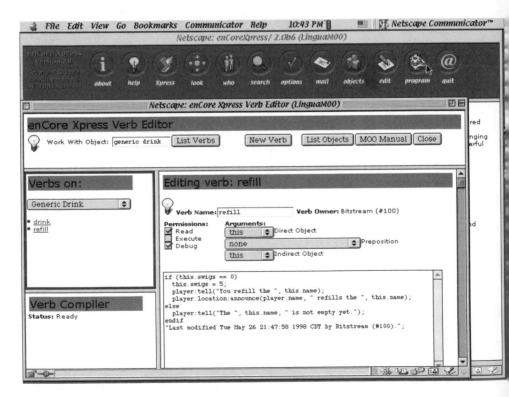

FIGURE 7.5   The enCore Xpress Verb Editor

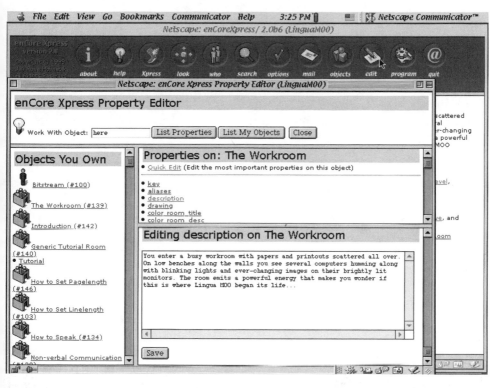

FIGURE 7.6   The enCore Xpress Property Editor

mented in the MOO's online help system. Below we'll only discuss a few of the commands that you will probably be using most frequently.

@display   This is a very useful command for listing names of verbs and properties on objects.

```
@display object:
```

Example: @display $thing:

Lists all object names on an object. Note that you must have a colon at the end of the command.

```
@display object.
```

Example: @display $thing.

Lists all property names on an object. Note that you must have a period at the end of the command.

@list   The list command is used to display verb code. This is very useful when you want to take a closer look at how verbs in the MOO are actually written.

```
@list object:verb
```

Example: @list $player:tell

@rmverb   Use this verb to delete verbs you no longer want.

```
@rmverb object:verb
```

Example: @rmverb MyObject:old_verb

@rmprop   Similar to the previous verb command, this one deletes properties.

```
@rmprop object.property
```

Example: @rmprop MyObject.some_property

@rename   In addition to renaming objects, this verb can also change verb names.

```
@rename object:verb_name to new_name
```

Example: @rename MyObject:test_verb to place

@renprop   This verb is only available in MOOs based on the enCore database and will allow you to change names of properties.

```
@renprop object.old_property_name to new_property_name
```

Example: @rename MyObject.taste to tastes

@args   This verb allows you to change the arguments of a verb after they have been defined.

```
@args object:verb indirect_object preposition direct_object
```

Example: @args MyObject:place this into any

@dump   Use this command to display the contents of all properties and code of all verbs on an object.

```
@dump object
```

Example: @dump MyObject

The MOO Utility Packages

The utility packages are collections of useful functions (verbs) that you may use in your programs. There are several such utility packages, but the most useful ones are probably the String Utilities ($string_utils), the List Utilities ($list_utils), the Time Utilities ($time_utils), the Object Utilities ($object_utils), and the Command Utilities ($command_utils). These utility packages are fairly well documented in the MOO's help system. To find out more about, for example, the Command Utilities, type *help $command_utils* in the MOO.

Built-In Functions

Like the utility packages, these are also useful functions that you can incorporate in your verbs. Help on these functions is available in the MOO by typing *help builtin*, and then typing *help* for the specific function you want to find out more about.

Fixing Bugs in Programs

No matter how careful you are when writing your MOO verbs, there will most likely be bugs in your code. These bugs can arise from a simple typo such as a colon in a place where a semicolon should be, or they can stem from logical or structural problems with your program. It is impossible to give a recipe on how to find and fix these bugs, but the MOO will help you by providing some pointers that may lead you to the answer.

The MOO checks for bugs at two different times. The first time is when you compile your verb. If it finds any errors in the code syntax, it will tell you in which line the error occurs. The second time is at runtime, that is, when you execute the verb. If it finds a bug at this time, it will produce what is called a *trace back* pointing you to the verb and line in which the bug occurred. It will also give you a pointer as to what kind of error it detected.

When bugs occur, you must go back to your code and study it carefully. When you think you have found a problem, recompile your code again. You need to repeat this process until your verb works flawlessly. It might be a good idea to show your code to other programmers to get their opinion on what the problem is.

As you become more experienced it will be easier to avoid bugs as well as detect them, but never expect to be able to write programs that are bug-free right away. Fixing bugs is something all programmers must do no matter how experienced they are.

Sharing Your Generic Objects

One of the most satisfying things about MOO programming is watching other people have fun with objects based on generic objects that you create. If you would like to enable others to create new objects themselves based on your classes, you need to make your generic objects *fertile*, which means to allow them to have subclasses. The command for doing this is called *@chmod*, and here's what you must type to make your Generic Drink fertile:

```
@chmod "Generic Drink" +f
```

Before you make your objects fertile, you need to make sure that bugs and errors have been eliminated from your verbs so others don't run into problems using them.

Become a Hacker

In this chapter we have introduced you to the art of MOO programming, and to programming as writing. However, as we have indicated several times, the theory that we have talked about here can only be fully understood through programming practice. Therefore, it's vital that you use what you have learned as a springboard for creating new interactive objects. As a beginner it is always hard to understand the potential of what you can do with a programming language like MOO. Therefore, it is often helpful to look at what others have done to get inspiration. In the MOO, almost every verb can be read by anyone with a programmer bit, and this is something you should take advantage of. By using the *@display* and *@list* commands as described above, you can inspect which verbs are defined on various objects you come across and list their code to see how they are written. This should provide you with lots of pointers about how you can implement your own ideas.

Contrary to what most people think, hackers are not evil-minded programmers who are out to break into any bank, government, or military computer they find. Instead, hackers are devoted programmers who delight in sharing code and learning from one another. So, become a hacker, learn from other programmers' code, and share your own code. Before you know it, you have not only found new knowledge about MOO programming, but also new friends to share your hobby with.

Checklist for MOO Programmers

- Plan your new object through a process of abstraction and determine what preexisting class you want to base it on.

- Determine what the most general and abstract characteristics of your object are.
- Write down a list of verbs and properties that you'll need to represent those characteristics.
- Create your new generic object (@*create*).
- Plan what your verbs are supposed to do by outlining them in pseudocode.
- Add new verbs and make sure you get the verb arguments right (@*verb*).
- Add new properties and make sure you give them correct data types (@*property*).
- Program your verbs.
- Fix bugs.

The MOO programming language is far too complex to cover in one chapter, so if you want to go beyond the basics that we have discussed here, we encourage you to take a look at Pavel Curtis's *MOO Programmers Manual*, which is available online. The programmer's manual is very comprehensive and detailed, but may seem a bit daunting for new MOO programmers. If you find that the programmer's manual is too much to handle right away, we recommend instead that you take a look at Judy Anderson's excellent MOO programming tutorial (also known as *yduJ's Wind-Up Duck Tutorial*). For further information about object-oriented programming in general, we invite you to check out the abundance of books now available on this subject, either in your local library or favorite bookstore.

NOTES

1. Jan Rune Holmevik. *Educating the Machine: A Study in the History of Computing and the Construction of the SIMULA Programming Language.* Trondheim: Center for Technology and Society, 1994.
2. For those who may be familiar with the Java programming language, verbs are the same as methods, and properties are the same as variables.

CLASS DISCUSSION

Discuss how programming can be considered "writing" in the new virtual literacies to which you have been introduced in *MOOniversity*. Consider how it compares to writing in the traditional sense, and propose ways that it can be considered writing in a new cyphertextual sense. Discuss whether and how MOO programming should be evaluated in a writing class (or other type of course).

EXERCISES

1. Use the Generic class that you created in this chapter to create other drinks with different tastes.

2. Use your experience from the programming example to create a new class called Generic Food, complete with verbs and properties.

3. Create a new room that can be a café or a bar where people can interact with your new objects.

4. To learn more about programming in the MOO, read and do the exercises in Judy Anderson's *Wind-Up Duck Tutorial*.

REFERENCES AND FURTHER READINGS FOR MOO PROGRAMMERS

Judy Anderson. *yduJ's MOO Programmer's Tutorial*. Internet: http://www.cs.reading.ac.uk/people/mkh/virtual_worlds/MOO/tutorials/ducktutorial.html

Pavel Curtis. *MOO Programmers Manual*. Internet: ftp://ftp.lambda.moo.mud.org/pub/MOO/ProgrammersManual_toc.html

CHAPTER

8

MOO Classes, Research, and Publication

Virtual Classrooms

Now that you have learned the finer points of MOOing, and you have practiced quite a lot on your own, in this chapter you will learn how to maximize the potential of MOOing for educational purposes. In other words, it's time to MOO in the classroom! The question is: Which classroom? The beauty of learning in MOOspace is that it takes the notion of classroom and redefines the meaning of that term and the boundaries of classroom space. It also undoes the meaning of classtime. Time and distance have historically served as fixed limitations in educational institutions. Students have to come from a distance, whether from across the street or across the globe, in order to attend classes. Not only that, but students have to come when the school determines the time classes should meet. Therein lies the beauty of using a MOO to push those boundaries back. In some instances, students only meet in MOOspace, never meeting each other or the teacher F2F (face-to-face). At the time of this writing, those classes are rare and experimental. More often than not, you will encounter MOOs in your education as supplemental spaces to the traditional classroom. In this chapter you will learn more about why and what you can do in the virtual classroom.

Chances are that your class already meets in a networked computer classroom, or that your class meets frequently in a similar computer lab. Either way more and more teachers are taking advantage of the Internet and taking their classes online. In the beginning (and perhaps every time), you will probably log on to the MOO during your regular classtime and with your entire class physically in the same computer classroom or lab. At first this may seem odd. Why would you need to meet in MOOspace at all when you are all present right in the physical classroom? Well, there are several reasons, and probably more we haven't discovered, but let's deal with what we know so far about how MOOs have enhanced teaching and learning.

Ok, you jump out of bed, running late as usual. You grab a cup of coffee at the student union and race to your writing class. Luckily today is the scheduled first trip to the MOO. You're thinking, "Great! I can ease my way into this thing because I'm not exactly wide awake yet. How hard can it be, right? I mean it's not like I have to *say* anything. And I didn't finish reading my assignment for today's discussion. I'll just hang out and let the talkers in class do all the talking." Soon everyone in class is logged on and you're learning the basics about talking and emoting. You think, "Hmmm...this is kind of fun. Not the usual boring lecture." Your teacher then explains that you need to break into your small groups to discuss the reading assignment. "But wait. Didn't she just say that she's recording the class? Didn't she say that anyone can see on the @*who* listing how long you've been idle (i.e., not talking)? Oh well, maybe if I just emote every now and then; you know, smile and nod a lot." Next thing you know, David is taking charge of your group, as usual. He's showing off not only how closely he read the assignment, but he's actually using some cool MOO features like *think bubbles, big signs,* and *stage talk.* Next thing you know you're drawn in by the multiple modes of interacting, you're talking openly about the assignment, voicing your take on it. Then it happens. Chen-li speaks. You've never heard her say anything in class, and the semester is half over! Not only that, but she has some great ideas. Other students notice, too, and begin to respond to her comments. Soon, the discussion has really taken off. You're no longer conscious of the fact that you're in MOOspace, or the fact that David and Chen-li are sitting just a few yards from you IRL (in real life). You find yourself caught up in the flow of conversation, several threads running at the same time. Some students talking about one aspect of the reading, others going off on other tangents, and you're glad that your teacher is logging it all. You want to be able to read it later and integrate some of the comments into your class project. It's quite a surprise, then, when the teacher says to the class that it's time to log off, classtime is over! Quickly your group decides to meet at the MOO later to pick up where you left off. David says he'll log on from home. Chen-li says she can use the lab in the library. You agree to meet her there so she can show you how to access the MOO outside the classroom. When you e-mail yourself the log of your group discussion before you log off you see that you all produced about 700 lines of text in one hour! Amazing! Then you look at your cup of coffee and realize it's still full and now cold. That, my friend, is the sign of a truly radical experience in class.

You see, it's difficult to characterize and define how different MOOspace is, and how beneficial and effective it is for educational purposes. Sometimes you just have to see for yourself. Imagine, then, the potential for students who *have* had their cup of coffee and who *have* read their assignments! Imagine your whole class having set their @*mood* to the way they *really* felt going into the class. This feature comes in handy because IRL you are limited to your physical demeanor to express your mental or emotional condition. But we're willing to bet that even if you had set your @*mood* to sleepy, by the end of that class you would change it to @*mood excited*!

```
@mood busy
You look busy.
who
Name                           Connected  Idle time  Location
----                           ---------  ---------  --------
Cynthia [busy] (#84) an hour              0 seconds  The Studio

Total: 1 player, who has been active recently.
@mood happy
You look happy.
who
Name                           Connected  Idle time  Location
----                           ---------  ---------  --------
Cynthia [happy] (#84) an hour             0 seconds  The Studio
```

In a sense, that's our challenge to you. Try it out for yourself. Check your skepticism at the virtual classroom door and try to be open about the possibilities for new and unique modes of learning and for meeting new and interesting people from all over the world. This last aspect of MOOing is causing some educators to rethink their own teaching, not to mention their own community of colleagues. Where else but a MOO could you literally "bump" into someone from Norway or Hong Kong while exploring your campus? That may not seem all that strange on your own campus if your school has lots of international students registered. But bumping into someone from Norway while they are still in Norway, now that borders on the impossible. Not only could you encounter such people, but you could find yourself collaborating on projects with them as well (something we will deal with in more detail in Chapter 9).

Multitasking

Still another benefit to holding class in MOOspace is the capability for multitasking in real-time and for multichannel conversations. Often your teacher will plan several activities during classtime, and working at the MOO is an excellent way to engage in several activities at once. You may wonder how all of this translates into more productivity on your part and how your teacher will be able to give you credit for it, so let's take a look at these questions using a writing class as an example.

In a more traditional writing class, you are evaluated on your process of writing as well as on the "products" that result from your writing process—the essays you are assigned to write. But for most of you there is usually a portion of your overall grade in the course that comes from "class participation." Often this is determined by your attendance, being on time for class, actively participating in group and class discussions, attending teacher–student conferences, and things like that. In essence, teachers have no "product" to evaluate when it comes to activity, so this portion of your grade is less quantifiable than the actual grades you make on your essays. The problem is that our system of evaluation is based on product more than process, and process more than activity. But some educators are trying to change the system. Using a model of evaluating children's activity, Peg Syverson of the University of Texas at Austin has created what she calls an "Online Learning Record" (OLR) that not only chronicles your activities online, it introduces a real and tangible way for you to participate in the grading process. We won't go into detail here about how the OLR works, but you can check it out on the WWW at the Web page shown in Figure 8.1.

Okay, so you understand some of how your activity at the MOO will contribute to your overall grade in the class. Now let's discuss what some of these activities online during class may be. We mentioned the fact that working in the MOO allows you to multitask and hold multiconversations. Some of you may be cringing at this potential, and some of you will find the possibility exciting. We know that there are many different learning styles, and we would not think of pigeonholing you into a mode of learning you are not comfortable with or ready for. As with any new mode of learning, you will have to experiment with the possibilities on the MOO before you settle into a comfortable and productive working style. The key is to realize your limitations, but also to learn about the MOO's capabilities before you chart your own path among the various options available to you.

Multitasking is actually not something you are unfamiliar with, although you may have never used that term to define what you do in class. Put simply, *multitasking* means you do more than one thing at a time. Of course we do not mean that you can do two or more things simultaneously, but close to it. It's like driving a car. At any given moment you are pressing the accelerator with your foot, steering the car with your hands, glancing in your rearview mirror to check on things behind you, reading signs on the road, talking to someone in the car with you, listening to the radio, talking on the phone, eating fast food on the way to class...well, you get the point. You are multitasking all the time in situations on a daily basis. Why should it be any different in class? Even when you are not in a computer classroom,

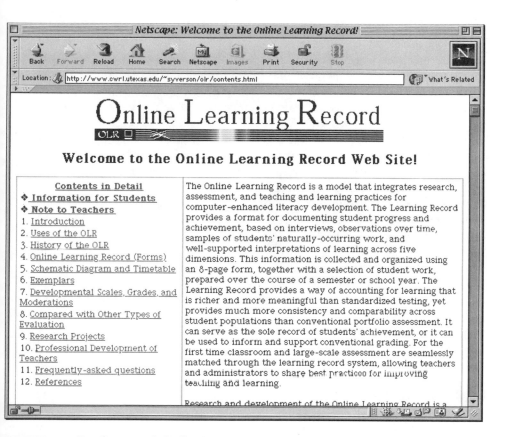

FIGURE 8.1   Peg Syverson's Online Learning Record

you multitask to some degree in class. You may be reading something in your textbook at the same time you are listening to your teacher. You might take notes while listening to a speaker in class, or consult your syllabus for next week's assignment as you raise your hand with another question, all the while thinking about what you're doing that evening with your friends. Multitasking is part of our way of life. So, in one sense, you need not worry that multitasking on a computer will be difficult to master. Just remember how you learned to drive a car. One day it will all became automatic.

Let's give some examples of how you can use the MOO to multitask during class. Suppose your assignment is to build your own room on the MOO, but you are also supposed to post to your class collective journal before the class ends. Simple. Open your word processing program and situate the window so that you can click from the MOO window to the word file and back again easily. Use your word window to draft both your room description and your journal entry. No need to open a separate file, just split them on the same page. After you create your room according to the instructions outlined earlier in this book, *@go* there and hang out while you switch to your word window. Now, take a stab at describing the room you created. If you get stuck, move below and start a paragraph that will become your class journal entry for that day. Ooops, you see that someone has paged you in your room at the MOO, so you switch back to that window and reply. If you get too busy working on your room descriptions and journal entry in the word window, you'll know if someone pages you by turning on your page bell using the command *@pageo +bell.* You'll probably want to leave the bell on most of the time, especially if you become so adept at multitasking that you have more than several windows open on your computer at once. Once you finish your room description, and you've edited it easily in your word program (same for your journal entry), use the copy function of your word program, switch back to your MOO window, and use the paste function of your MOO client to paste it into the description $noteditor, or the Objects editor of enCore Xpress (see Chapter 5 on MOO editors). Do the same for posting your journal entry to your class journal board. Simple, huh? Pretty soon you will be quite adept at multitasking in any number of ways while in the MOO. The key to remember is that the MOO allows you to maintain as many tasks at once as you want, including conversing, to which we now turn.

Multiconversing: Class and Group Discussions

One of the best features about MOO classrooms (especially those programmed as the enCore specific classrooms are) is the ability to talk to one group or the whole group while also paging privately back and forth with people in the same MOO room as you, people in the same MOO, and people at other MOOs (if your MOO is linked via interMOO communication channels). But navigating your way through all the text scrolling across your screen can be very disorienting and often unwelcome. Again, different learning styles and personality types react to these features in various ways. But there are always ways to manage the input. For now, let's entertain the possibility for multiconversations, and we'll use the enCore classroom for this example.

The classroom is programmed to enable three groups to hold separate discussions with one another while in the same MOO room. In Figure 8.2 (Lingua MOO's C-FEST room), you have a worktable, at which two or more

C-FEST Forum

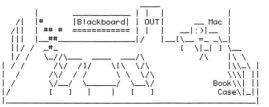

```
You enter an informally furnished room that is comfortable and full of
energy. In the center of the room is a table with a sofa on either side.
A cactus plant stands proudly beneath the *blackboard on the north wall,
and on the other side of the door is a worktable with a computer on it.
The room has the feel of housing a thinktank...educators who deliberate
'with' technology, debate 'delivery', and discuss new modes of presenting
research. Type 'look blackboard' for various instructions on links and objects
in this room.

You see Left Sofa, Right Sofa, and Worktable.
You see Equipment, CF Ideas Board, Recorder, CF Announcement, Chronicle Joblist,
Job Board, Conference Cabinet, Bad Blood, CF(3/4), and test.
You teleport into C-FEST Forum...
sit left
Cynthia sits down at Left Sofa. . .
"hi
Cynthia [to others at Left Sofa]: hi
su here's how you speakup
You speak up, "here's how you speakup"
```

FIGURE 8.2   C-FEST Moderated Room Session

may sit and converse. And you have two other sofas at which two more groups may do likewise. The *say* and *emote* commands work at these stations as if the sofa or table itself is a room. If you talk normally, only those seated where you are will see what you say.

However, if you "speakup" to the whole class, as you may be asked to do from time to time, you have another say command that enables you to *speakup* (*speakup text* or *su text* for short). This might take some getting used to, but used effectively it can serve to use classtime so much more productively than in a so-called *real* classroom series of discussions. Imagine trying to do this IRL. You have three groups physically split into three circles of chairs, and you hear three groups of conversations going. Suddenly someone speaks louder and addresses the whole classroom, which causes everyone to look up and conversation to stop in all groups. Sometimes we see teachers doing this, but mostly as a way of giving further instructions to the whole class or letting everyone in the groups know that the class is ending. But if you have the ability to hold more than one group discussion *and* contribute to a class discussion without disrupting the individual group discussions, it enriches the level of discussion overall. Combine this capability with the periodic private pages you receive from your classmates, your teacher, and/or other players in the MOO, and you have a rich multiconversation going.

If this seems disorienting, there are ways to manage the overwhelming amount of text you see. Learning to filter through the text takes practice and patience, but it is certainly possible. Sometimes you may want to capture the session and read it all later when you can slow things down to your own pace of reading and typing. Or you may want to use a different room for your group discussion in order to filter out the other comments that students "speakup." Just remember that learning anything new carries a certain amount of frustration with it. Let your teacher know if you have problems, and she or he will help you resolve them.

More than likely your teacher will not expect you to be able to multitask and multiconverse right away. We're all beginners at some time or another. You will have the chance to participate in class discussions or demonstrations of the MOO, learning at a modest pace the basic commands for talking, emoting, and moving around in the MOO. Once your class is comfortable with the basics, your teacher will move on to more advanced activities and may begin recording your class and individual group discussions. The ability to record and archive transcripts like class discussions may not seem new or innovative. After all, tape recorders and video cameras have served this purpose for years, though teachers use them only in special circumstances (and in certain disciplines). Figure 8.3 shows a peer editing session in which students work together on a draft of a paper.

What makes MOO logs of class discussions beneficial varies from situation to situation, but in general we think there are two important reasons: (1) the ability to capture spontaneous and productive discussion that would otherwise be lost when not recorded, and (2) the ability to reread the transcript for the purposes of rhetorical analysis. To understand how you contribute to a socially constructed discussion on a given topic is a valuable lesson. To analyze how discussions are socially constructed is another. Rhetoric is not just about speaking or writing. It is also about social interaction and the social construction of knowledge. Recording sessions between two or more people on the MOO facilitates these lessons in ways we did not have before. But the MOO is also a powerful tool for individuals working on their own, both during class and outside of class. When you begin to use the MOO by yourself, you will find it as conducive a place to study and research as your school library.

Individual Learning

Have you ever been reading a book in the library, making notes and studying toward a research project? Sure, we all have. And have you ever found yourself at home, and you realize you forgot to write down the reference information for your bibliography, or something equally important? Yes, been there,

```
●  ▭▭▭▭▭▭▭▭▭▭▭▭ Lingua MOO ▭▭▭▭▭▭▭▭▭▭▭ ◱ ◳
Logan arrives.                                                          ▲
Julian arrives.                                                        ▝
Cynthia says, "ok, we need to work on Logan's paper today, right?"
Julian says, "yes, we worked on my paper and Pamela's before the break."
Logan says, "right"
"thanks for all the good feedback on mine. Now I have some specifics to go on when I'm
revising
You say, "thanks for all the good feedback on mine. Now I have some specifics
 to go on when I'm revising"
Cynthia says, "has everyone read Logan's draft?"
Julian says, "I have"
"me too
You say, "me too"
Cynthia says, "ok, who wants to paste in something from Logan's draft to
 discuss?"
Julian says, "I have a passage I didn't quite get, so I'll paste it in now"
--------------------------------Julian--------------------------------
When you are a victim of a hate crime, it makes you question what kind of
 country/world you live in.  Everyone knows that there are bad people in the
 world and that bad things happen to good people.  However, when someone
 pinpoints you to hate because you are affiliated with a certain group, it
 makes you...  The only way I can describe it is that nothing makes sense any
 longer.  It is incomprehensible.  When someone broke into my storeroom last
 year and took everything I had, I was angry and I was guilty of wishing them
 ill.
"I think you need to finish that one sentence in the middle. And that last sentence
sounds strange to end on the word "ill." Maybe a different word?
You say, "I think you need to finish that one sentence in the middle. And that
 last sentence sounds strange to end on the word "ill." Maybe a different
 word?"
─────────────────────────────────────────────────────────────────────
$
```

FIGURE 8.3   **Peer Editing Session**

done that. Have you ever worked online in your computer classroom during class, searching the WWW for resources on your paper topic? Some of you have, no doubt. And have you ever reached home and realized you don't have access to the same computer as in your classroom where you bookmarked that Web site, and now you need it badly? OK, we've all experienced these moments when our work hits a snag because we work in so many places that it becomes hard to keep track of our sources, to manage our methodologies, to record our own intellectual footprints. That's where the MOO comes in.

As we explained in Chapter 2, if you have Internet access, you have access to a MOO. Granted, many of you do not have access from home, but the majority of post-secondary schools (and many public libraries) have computers with Internet access. Consult with your teacher or the academic computing services department on your campus to find out how to gain access. And now that you have learned the basics of MOOing, either find a quiet spot in your favorite educational MOO to work, or if you have a player account, settle into your own virtual room or office. But you don't exactly know what to do now. You may even feel foolish sitting there idling. In order to begin to think differently about how you work and where, we'll give you an example and then let you try out a few of your own.

Let's back up a bit and replay the library scenario. Instead of sitting in the library, Mark decides to check out the books he needs and heads to the campus computer lab. Once there, he puts in a floppy disk and opens the word processing program on the computer. Now he has a blank document ready for taking notes as he reads. Next, Mark logs in to the campus network and opens his e-mail program, careful to move that window to the side so that he can toggle between his word file and his e-mail window. He remembers that early in the semester his teacher had e-mailed the class with a list of online citation format sources and some other WWW sites of interest, and he may need to look that up. Mark is writing a paper on post cold-war economics, and he found few resources at the library because this topic is so current. As he reads, he comes across a reference to something he had heard about on National Public Radio (NPR) that morning. He decides to log on to the MOO to see if any of his group from class happens to be online. Maybe they heard it too. After he logs on, Mark checks who is online with @*who*. To his relief he sees that Maria is online and she's talking to another member of the class in the MOO classroom. Mark pages Maria and asks whether she happened to hear the morning NPR program. She pages back that she did and invites Mark to join her and Natalie. Mark teleports into the MOO classroom, waves to Natalie and Maria, and says, "Thanks, Maria. I'm working on this paper, and on NPR they interviewed some Harvard economist and I need to cite the interview and include some of her comments." Maria says, "Cool, did you know that NPR has a Web site and that you can find transcripts of their news program, 'All Things Considered,' and also listen to some of the interviews via Real Audio? You can even download the audio file to your computer from the WWW and play it back as many times as you want." Mark exclaims, "No way! The problem is that I'm on a computer in the lab on campus. And I need to be able to take notes while I listen because I'll not be able to access it from home." To which Maria suggests, "Well, if I were you I would @*create* a $note here at the MOO, then go into the text editor with @*notedit* and get ready to type into that window while you listen to the interview. Take notes onto your newly created $note, save it, and then if you want, you can continue working on that same note in class tomorrow when we log on to the MOO. You can even encrypt the note so that no one else can read it. You can e-mail yourself the note or read it while in the MOO and copy and paste text from your MOO window directly into your word file that is your actual paper." Mark exclaims again, "Really!? That's a great idea!" Then Natalie chimes in, saying, "Another way would be to paste the WWW URL address for the audio interview into a $webprojector on the MOO. Then tomorrow in class you can display it for the class all at once and we can all listen to it together and give you our feedback as well." Mark says, "Thanks to both of you. This is great. Ciao! See you tomorrow!"

The key to remember in this scenario is that access to the MOO and other Internet programs like e-mail and the WWW may be easily accessible on campus outside of classtime, but the MOO conversation between Mark and Maria and Natalie pulled it all together for Mark. If they had all met IRL in the library, for instance, it is possible that Maria had heard that same interview, and she might even had been able to share the WWW address for NPR with Mark. But how to help him capture his notes while listening and how to make those notes available in class the next day would have been almost impossible without the MOOspace where Mark can take notes, e-mail himself those notes, print them out on the spot if he wants, set up a $webprojector slide for enabling the whole class to listen to the interview as a point of discussion—only on a MOO is it possible for synchronous (real-time) and asynchronous ($notes, slides, e-mail, or WWW) activities to take place in one workspace.

Of course, we can think of countless scenarios like this one, but you get the general idea. Even when no one else is logged on to the MOO, you have access to a powerful workspace, thinktank, personal archive, collaboration tools, research network, and presentation equipment, among other things. The possibilities are almost endless, and often MOO administrators will work with you if you have an idea for a tool or object that could help them work more effectively. For example, recently a graduate student from the University of Texas at Dallas wanted to set up a series of linked "rooms" at Lingua MOO that contained a twenty-page seminar paper for a course on "Virtual Rhetorics." Denise wanted her classmates, and other Lingua users, to be able to read her paper by moving from room to room. The text of the paper is pasted into each room description so that the player finds herself "inside" Denise's paper. But Denise wanted to know *what* her readers thought as they read; she wanted feedback on her research, in other words. We suggested that she create simple recorders for each "room" of her paper and drop the recorder and turn it on, leaving it on all the time. She would include an instruction $note in the initial room that guides the reader and invites their comments as they read. All they have to do is talk in any room that they happen to have comments about. The recorder captures all comments and who makes them. Denise thought about this for a minute, then asked, "But what if I want to respond to someone's specific comment? How can I (or anyone for that matter) read the accumulating text in a given room and respond?" We then suggested that we nix the recorder idea and create chain-story $notes in each room that are writable by any reader/player and that appends their name to their comments. Voila! That was exactly what Denise wanted. Now her readers could add their comments without having to read everything else others had written before them, or without having to talk openly (which can be disconcerting if other readers happen to be in the same room). Of course having other readers in the same room can also result in interesting feedback in the form of conversations among readers. Add Denise herself to the mix (if she logs on as well and joins them), and you have a unique real-time interchange among real players/authors/readers in addition to the text of the paper itself and the accumulated comments of other players who have come before.

What we have described is also an example of using the MOO as a workspace and research archive. But it can be so much more as well. In the MOO the sky's the limit, your imagination's the limit, and the limit is permeable and ever-changing. There are many specially programmed educational MOO tools available to you and your teacher, and we have mentioned a few of them in these few examples about individual learning. In the remaining section of this chapter we will suggest ways to use these tools for publication, presentations, and special events.

Publish Web Pages in the MOO

Web-based MOO access systems like enCore Xpress highlight the power of integrating writing for the WWW with synchronous interactivity. While the MOO does not offer complete instructions on writing and designing Web pages, with a few simple steps you can create your own Web page in the MOO making it possible to publish your own writing. In enCore-based MOOs, for example, it is possible to publish entirely customized Web pages just as you would on any other Web server. This is made possible by a special room called $webpage.

To publish a fully customized Web page in the MOO, create a new room, change its parent from $room to $webpage, and enter or paste the HTML code for the page into the description of the Web page room. If you are using the Xpress client, click on the Objects button to open the Objects Editor window, click on *create,* and select the $webpage room. For best results when designing Web pages, we recommend that you use a graphical Web editor. Note that any images that you embed in your page must be uploaded to a regular Web server.

A Web page room can be read either with a Web browser complete with external links and all the elements you choose to embed, or from inside the MOO. When viewed inside the MOO, all HTML code on the Web page is filtered out, and external links and other elements are disabled.

Presentational Tools and Special Events

So far in this chapter you have seen how classes and individuals are using educational MOOs to supplement the traditional classroom experience and the traditional individual learning process. As we have stressed from the beginning, MOOs are learning environments that serve students and teachers in a number of innovative ways. So, it shouldn't come as a surprise to learn that using the MOO is also a splendid mode of presentation of writing and research or as a place ideally suited for holding meetings, panels, poetry readings, and other special events. The fact that the MOO is a multiuser domain means that with some promotion and organization, you have a ready-made real-time audience. Basically, the MOO is an excellent place to present what you have learned and to organize special events where guest speakers discuss various topics with your audience, or where your group presents their research project, or where creative works like poetry or fiction are "recited" to an audience of your peers and/or other MOO players from all over the world. The question is how to go about organizing presentations and special events.

You are probably used to making class presentations the old-fashioned way. You stand before the class, speaking extemporaneously from notes, reading a paper, or reciting from memory. If you're like us, these situations can create anxiety galore. Other conventional methods of presentation utilize transparencies and overhead projectors, slides, and, more recently, videotapes or computer projections of PowerPoint-type presentations. The MOO offers a way to diminish the anxiety and present projects in a variety of ways to a variety of audiences.

Two of the simplest ways to deliver your ideas or texts don't require much preparation at all, and if you are using a MOO on which you are only a guest, chances are these are your best options. On the MOO you can use "big signs" or the @paste function to call your MOO audience's attention to your text. For example, if you are in class and are asked to give an impromptu summary of a project you are working on, a quick way to get everyone's attention is to hold up a big sign like this:

```
                                 _____
                                |                         |
Jesse holds up a BIG sign:      | What number were we on  |
                                |_____|
sar says, "8"
Stallion asks, "Should women be allowed to serve in the
military?????"
```

This works best if you type fairly well and quickly, skills that will certainly be improved the more you MOO. Because it may not be possible to paste in pretyped text in a spontaneous situation like that, just enter *bb* and the text you want to say (it's best to keep it brief and hold up several big signs rather than one long one). Then once you have the class's attention, you can dispense with using the big signs and just talk.

The other simple way to give an impromptu summary of your project is to use the @paste feature. As explained in Chapter 4, you can paste in text from another file like a word processing file or some other text file that you have open in addition to your MOO window. Or, if you have a player account on the MOO, you can also *@paste* in text from files you store in the MOO itself. Usually these are $notes you have created for papers or any text you are working on. In the first instance, you just copy a selection of text (keep it brief, no more than about ten to fifteen lines) from your text file, and in your MOO window type *@paste,* then hit return. The MOO prompts you at this point for your text, and you then select the paste feature of your MOO client and the text appears in your window. You must then type a "." on a line by itself, and hit return again. The text will now appear in the display of all players in that MOO room. If you are pasting in text from a file you are carrying on your player, you need only to *read* that file and have it display on your own screen in order to select the section you want, use the MOO client's copy function to copy, type *@paste,* hit return, then use the paste function of your MOO client to paste in the text. Enter a "." on a line by itself and hit return. The text now appears in all players' screens just as any text from a non-MOO file. Simple and fast! But what about more elaborate and dynamic presentations? For those you need a player account and some preparation time and presentation practice.

Among the other options for presentation of text you want to consider are MOO Slides, $webprojector slides, MOO videos, recitable notes, lecture devices, and notice boards. You might even want to get really creative and create a *bot* to present for you, or to interact with you based on keywords you program it to respond to.

1. MOO Slides (see Figure 8.4) are especially appropriate for snippets of text that you display in order to generate discussion between slides. Keep in mind that each slide projector holds ten MOO Slides that hold about twenty lines of text each. We recommend that you limit the amount of text on each slide, however, because large blocks of text are difficult to read if players are talking and emoting between slides. MOO Slides are easily prepared ahead of time and cut down on the typo factor. All you do is prompt each slide when you're ready. You may even review them on your own screen prior to showing them to the whole group.

2. MOO $webprojector slides are a bit more complicated, but only in the sense that in order for all players in your audience to see the Web page you project with the slide, everyone including you must be logged on to the MOO via a Web-based access system, like enCore Xpress, using Netscape or another Web browser.

3. In enCore-based MOOs, you may also use the Xpress client to display Web pages with the simple *@url* command. When you type @url http:// whatever.com the Web window of the screen will display the page. This works well for impromptu occasions for presenting, as well as for a few displays. Using the $webprojector is best for more than a few slides prepared in advance.

BusyBee shows slide #8.

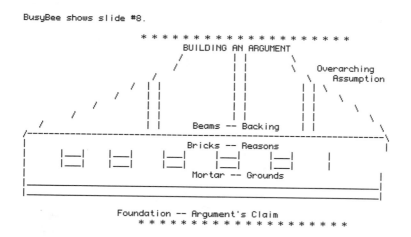

```
        * * * * * * * * * * * * * * * * * * * *
               BUILDING AN ARGUMENT
              /          | |         \
            /       | |         \    Overarching
          /       | |         \  \   Assumption
        /   |  |       | |        | | \
      /   /  |  |     | |       | |   \
    /   /  |  |      | |       | |    \
  /   /   |  |      | |      | |    \
 /   /    |  |   Beams -- Backing | |     \
/------------------------------------------------\
|          |  |  Bricks -- Reasons          |
|  |—|  |—|    |—|  |—|  |—|    |          |
|  |—|  |—|    |—|  |—|  |—|    |          |
|                Mortar -- Grounds            |
|_____|
|_____|

        Foundation -- Argument's Claim
          * * * * * * * * * * * * * * * * * * *
```

FIGURE 8.4   MOO Slide Sample

4. Videos are a creative way to stage a more dynamic presentation that is especially useful if you want to move around in the MOO as you prepare your presentation and if you want to "play" back the experience "as if" you are viewing it as it happened. To create a video you need to first create a Video recorder, a TV, and a VCR to view and play it on, then the tape. Once you have the video taped, you then drop the TV and VCR in the room, hook the VCR up to the TV, load the tape in the VCR, and turn the VCR on. The other players will then see a steadily paced video of text reenacting exactly what you taped beforehand. Here is a brief shot of what you see when you play back the Lingua MOO Grand Opening from April, 1995:

```
turnon tv
Cynthia turns on TV.
play 5 on tv
Cynthia selects the tape <<Lingua MOO Grand Opening>> for
viewing..

[on TV]      Cynthia says, "Welcome to Lingua MOO!"

[on TV]      Cynthia says, "I'm Cynthia Haynes of UTD, and
this is Jan Rune Holmevik, of Oslo, Norway."

[on TV]      Cynthia says, "We're your hosts for today, and
we want to thank you for coming to the opening."

[on TV]      Cynthia says, "Now I would like to turn things
over to Jan who will give us a little background on
Lingua..."

[on TV]      Jan says, "Thank you, Cynthia"
```

[on TV]   Jan says, "LinguaMOO was founded a little over
two months ago, in January this year."

[on TV]   Jan says, "It is the result of a collaboration
between Cynthia and me, a collaboration that really started
last summer when we first met on MediaMOO and later Meridian."

[on TV]   Jan says, "At that time we were both working on
our theses and spent a fair amount of time together online."

[on TV]   Jan says, "It was during this time that we first
conceived of the idea of writing an article together about
collaboration in MOOspace."

5. Recitable $notes are fairly simple to create and are excellent for reciting poetry, short fiction, and anything else that works best displayed at three to five second intervals. Be sure, however, that if you plan to prompt a recitable note that your audience is asked to remain quiet during the recitation. If not, the recitation will be interrupted by text from talking and emoting players.

6. The lecture device is especially nice for somewhat lengthier texts like poems or short stories. The beauty of a lecture device is that it looks exactly like you are saying it at the moment, when in reality you have pasted the text written offline into the device in advance. To effectively do this, you need to make sure to paste in the text line by line as you would be "speaking" it in the MOO, or else long chunks of text spill forth at too short intervals to read it all. Plus, the gig is up and your audience realizes you aren't really "saying" it in real-time. Or are you? The lecture device can be programmed to different intervals and cuts down on the error and typing speed factors as well.

7. Notice boards are also relatively easy to use as presentation tools and have the added feature of allowing your audience to post comments of their own to the board. This tool would work well if you have an annotated outline type presentation, or a series of steps that build on one another. Boards that you own may be set up to accommodate other player contributions or not, as you see fit. Once you drop a Notice Board object in a MOO room, however, you must instruct the players to read each notice individually. But this can also work well if you want to hold a discussion between each entry. Notice Boards can also serve as project boards for your own benefit. If asked to discuss your project, just bring your board along to the MOO classroom and drop it for your teacher and/or other students to read.

8. Bots require more advanced building and programming skills, but can be used quite creatively for presentation of research. A well-versed bot, programmed with keywords you select, could be used for impromptu dialogues that you hold with yourself in front of others, or they could be used to

answer questions that you anticipate receiving once your presentation is over. For example, after showing a series of MOO slides, or a video presentation, your teacher asks the audience if they have questions. You could program your bot to answer these questions in advance if you have crafted your presentation to evoke certain predictable questions. You could then even hold a conversation with your bot as if it is occurring spontaneously. Of course you must remember the keywords your bot will respond to and not slip up and repeat a word at a time you don't want the bot to reply. But, then again, that could be a humorous way to engage your audience as well.

For special events, the MOO presentational objects we have described above may be used throughout the event, but you also need to know about the various MOO rooms best suited for special events and some examples of what a special event is. As we mentioned earlier in this chapter, using MOOs in teaching is rapidly creating the need for educators to rethink how they evaluate students' activities online. Before you jump into the idea feet first, however, you should definitely consult your teacher about the possibility of organizing an "event" at the MOO. Just as any RL meeting, poetry reading, or symposium, hosting a MOO event requires planning and implementation down to the last detail. We encourage you to consider such a project, but we caution you not to think that a MOO event is in any way less work than a RL event project.

For example, let's say Mark (our student working on a paper on post cold-war economics) decides to conduct a panel on the MOO and invite some graduate students studying postwar political science, history, and sociology to hold a roundtable discussion on this topic. First Mark obtains permission from his teacher to include the MOO event as part of the portfolio work for this project. Then he checks with the MOO administrators for advice about where to post announcements (like various Bulletin Boards and *general lists). They will help Mark determine what space on the MOO is available for the event he is planning, whether or not he needs his panelists to have player accounts, and they will advise him about the best ways to promote the event. He should also check with the MOO administrators about the various moderated rooms available for the kind of event he is planning. In this example, we'll say Mark chooses the Auditorium (a special room available in all enCore MOOs). The Auditorium is perfect for the event Mark is planning because the panelists are "sitting" on a stage and cannot see the comments of the audience until the moderator (Mark) pops out a question that an audience member has asked. The audience may talk all they want and see both what the panelists say and what the other players say and emote. A further mode of filtering talk is also available to audience members by donning a special "headset" that now allows only what the panelists say to come through. As Mark familiarizes himself with how the room works, he thinks through how this room meets the needs of the event, making sure to test each feature listed in the help text for the room.

For example, Mark checks out how to setup the program that the audience and panelists will see on entering the room. With the help of a friend or a secondary test character he logs on with, Mark might run some test questions through the moderator system so that he understands how to instruct the audience to queue questions to the panelists. It is also important to record the event, so Mark learns how to work the recording system in the Auditorium, or if it has none, he *@creates* one for himself and tests how to use it, always recycling his test tape when he finishes. Now the designated room is all set.

Next, he composes a MOOmail to the *general mailing list (or *events at some MOOs) announcing the call for participation (to solicit the graduate student panelists). Mark might also post the call to some selected e-mail discussion listservs that would draw panelists from outside his own school. After he confirms who his panelists will be, Mark selects a date and time to hold the event at the MOO, preferably a time suitable and sensitive to the time zones of his panelists. Now Mark writes a series of questions or prompts for discussion and contacts his panelists detailing what he hopes they will discuss and how. For those panelists new to MOOing, Mark needs to write up a brief beginner's guide to MOOing (or he requests permission from the MOO administrators to forward any help sheets they have ready to hand) for the panelists, and he provides a series of rehearsal times so the panelists can learn the basics of talking, emoting, and moving around.

As part of his project, Mark could also keep a project board handy in his own MOO room, checking off the various to-do items as he completes them prior to the event itself. For events like this, MOO administrators are often willing to place a special welcome message on the login screen announcing the event and what to type in order to *@go* to the designated MOO room. This helps new users log on easily and find their way quickly to the room. Finally, Mark should prepare his questions using one of the presentational tools discussed in the previous section of this chapter, and then he e-mails his panelists with the final instructions about what to expect.

Mark might also want to line up some MOO helpers from his own classmates, students who assist the panelists and/or the MOO audience who may have trouble with the technology at first. They could log on as, say, "Natalie-helper," or something like that. As the event begins, Mark should open by welcoming everyone and announcing that the event will be recorded (*before* he turns on the recorder). And he should then turn on the recorder and prompt his first slide (or big sign, lecture device, or whatever presentation object he chooses to use for the prompts). This slide should inform the audience of the basic rules for asking questions, for how to "sit" in the room, and so forth. Another way to accomplish this would be to place all instructions on a blackboard object in the room. Mark could then hold up a big sign instructing everyone to *read blackboard*, they all do so at their own prompting, and Mark gets the ball rolling by prompting the panelists with their first discussion question. As the event winds down, Mark should thank everyone for coming and turn off the recorder. If he decides to make the transcript available, Mark could then hold up a big sign with the URL address of the log (provided the MOO has a Web interface similar to enCore MOOs).

This is just one example of the type of event that could be organized at a MOO. We have seen students coordinate poetry readings, put on MOO plays, moderate panels of expert panelists on Faulkner (for example), host short-fiction readings, organize a series of meetings in semimoderated rooms (like C-FEST or the Kairos e-journal "Meet the Author" series, both of which meet at Lingua MOO), short demos or MOO tours of projects, like the paper Denise set up as a matrix of MOO rooms, and so forth. The list could go on and on. The key is that MOO presentations and special events open doors that would not otherwise be available to students. Isn't it time for you to open one of those doors?

CLASS DISCUSSION

1. Compare RL multitasking to online multitasking and discuss. How do they compare? What do you notice about how you react to RL juggling of multiple conversations, projects, deadlines, and so on? Are you comfortable with having multiple windows open on your computer? What are the advantages and disadvantages in learning to multitask with MOOs?

2. Discuss advantages and disadvantages between moderated classrooms and generic rooms in terms of how they restrict discussion or not. What kinds of situations would benefit from moderated discussion? From unmoderated discussion?

3. Discuss pros and cons of the integration of MOO and WWW technology. What design issues relate to writing both in the MOO and the WWW? How important are graphical interfaces to learning, in your view?

4. Discuss other presentational tools that you would like to see implemented on a MOO. Use your imagination! Keep in mind that MOO administrators and teachers are usually open to suggestions from student players. If you have a suggestion, send it to your teacher as well as the wizard list of the MOO. (If you are really enterprising, and you have learned how to program using Chapter 7, for extra credit program your own presentational tool.)

5. Discuss how artificial intelligence (like bots) relates to identity issues. What are the implications of using bots to interact with you and other MOO users? How could bots be used in interaction with other bots?

EXERCISES

1. Write an online class presentation using one of the presentational tools discussed in this chapter (i.e., lecture device, MOO Slides, $webprojector, etc.). Think in terms of writing assignments that could be formatted in other ways than a traditional essay, such as hypertext, a series of rooms or $notes, a prerecorded video tour of your textual project, and so forth.

2. Design a set of MOO rooms that can be browsed as hypertext. That is, use the MOO as a hypertext publication for a group of rooms or "texts." Create a way for readers of your texts to leave their comments (i.e., using a guest book, notice board, recorder, chain-story, etc.).

3. Create a bot and program it with keywords and record various interactions with the bot and other students or visitors to your MOO room. Attach a copy of the MOO log to your assignment.

4. Create a MOO video that gives a tour of the MOO to a new student. Be creative! Include spontaneous interaction with other persons who happen to be online while you are taping, in addition to your own comments as you narrate the video.

5. Create your own homepage on the MOO and refer to the information in this chapter about how to attach and display graphic files to MOO objects and MOO $webpage rooms. For a final presentation to your class, organize a tour of your site using a $webprojector and display your pages and related links while your class plays audience in your MOO room.

9 Collaboration on the MOO

In this chapter we explore the multi-user dimension that makes MOOs arguably one of the most powerful technologies for collaboration available. As we mentioned in Chapter 1, the recent proliferation of educational and professional MOOs has spawned a new generation of collaborative environments that puts people together from all areas of the world working on projects of all kinds. In your learning experience, you are probably more used to thinking of collaboration as what happens between two people coauthoring a paper or report, or as something that occurs in other disciplines than writing (like the sciences, for example). Our first task, then, in this chapter is to broaden the scope of what collaboration means. Next we will discuss why using MOOs to collaborate is a good idea and how to do so. Finally, we'll talk about a special case in which the use of MOOs for collaboration is rapidly entering the fields of language learning and English as a Second (or Foreign) Language.

What Is Collaboration in MOOspace?

By now you have some concrete MOO experience under your belt, some of which involved your class and some you obtained by exploring and learning about things on your own. We like to think of collaboration as broadly as possible. So first we ask that you consider the MOO itself (and those behind-the-scenes programmers and wizards) as your writing and learning partner. We're pretty sure that at some point in your initial exploration of the MOO and how it works, you typed some command and the MOO replied with "I don't understand that." Or let's say you entered a string command (one that contains more than one verb or argument) and you got the syntax wrong, so the MOO responds with, for example, "Try @notedit <object>.<property> instead." The MOO enters a dialogue with you from time to time. It "colabors" with you as you talk, emote, move around, build, or program, constantly cueing you when you make a wrong move or send a wrong command. You might even be trying to pick something up or go somewhere, and you see "Either that object doesn't want to go, or you can't accept it." Or, you see "@go Courtyard is ambiguous. Which courtyard do you mean?" In both cases the MOO talks back, gently reminding you that you are not alone completely, that your learning process, as all MOO users' processes, has been taken into account in the creation of the MOO database. It makes suggestions sometimes, or it simply tells you if it cannot understand your request. Try this in your word processing program, and you won't get very far. Your word program allows you to make mistakes, and it certainly doesn't make suggestions unless you have turned on the spellcheck and grammar features yourself (both of which are still limited in how much they help your writing). The significance of the MOO response is that it acts at times in collaboration with you in your learning process. It recognizes that learning how to use its commands requires a certain degree of guidance and cooperation. To think of the MOO environment as your partner increases the speed at which you learn and enhances the *way* you learn. It's a bonus that you also learn *more*. The key is that your increased productivity is driven by writing and reading in collaboration with the MOO itself.

Another way to broaden your concept of collaboration is to rethink what knowledge is and how it gets constructed. In Chapter 1 we talked a little about the social construction of knowledge and how virtual communities are first and foremost social communities; that is, their members form the conditions of possibility for social interaction that leads to new knowledge. In other words, in the MOO you don't necessarily have to be engaged in a project clearly defined as "collaborative" to be collaborating.

To give you an example of what we mean, let's say that, like Mark in our example in Chapter 8, you might be working alone online (during class or not) and you want to run something by someone right then and there. It doesn't matter if you're working on building, describing, mailing, or whatever; or, you might even be writing in a word file while leaving your MOO session window in the background. The point is that you aren't sure about something you have written, or you want to get some feedback on an idea. If you see friends, classmates, or teachers on the MOO (having called up the *@who* listing), you can page them and ask if they have time for a question or for reading something you have written. You can either *@paste* them the passage or sentence privately (especially if they are in a conversation with someone else in another part of the MOO), asking them to page you with their response, or you might just ask them to talk over an idea if they have time. Consulting others is a form of collaboration, whether they are your peers or not.

We speak from experience when we say that working at the MOO puts you in touch with potential collaborators of all kinds, and at times or the day when you would least likely be able to find one. As MOO administrators, we could not have built Lingua MOO without the help of many others; but, we also could not continue to maintain and improve the MOO without their help either. That's why one MOO administrator we mentioned earlier in the book, Gustavo Glusman of BioMOO, created a wizard channel for all the MOOs connected together through his GNA (Globewide Network Academy) net. The channel acts as a life support line almost, at times providing emergency help, at other times serving as a hotline for quick solutions to problems.

What we're saying is that "working together," i.e., co-laboring, should be a fundamental way of thinking about collaboration. If you study with one or more students in the library or student center at your school, or even if you are studying alone and periodically talk to others while you study, you might not think of that as collaboration. But you are working, are you not? The same holds true for working online at a MOO. Unfortunately, because of the gaming origins of MOOs, and because of the negative media attention we explained in Chapter 1, people often think that when you MOO, you are just "hanging out," loafing, or engaging in idle "chat." Of course people use MOOs for those reasons as well, but why let that become the primary perception of MOOs? Those things go on in libraries, too, and yet libraries enjoy a different kind of reputation. Educational MOOs are complete learning environments with the potential for collaboration and research, discussion and debate, and, yes, hanging out.

The rapid popularity of educational MOOs for writing instruction has contributed greatly to the legitimation of text-based synchronous learning, though many other disciplines are taking interest and creating their own MOOs. Interestingly, humanities subjects like rhetoric and composition have been pioneers in the collaborative learning movement, recognizing the power of students teaching each other. The writing process is clearly improved, according to composition scholars, by collaborative input. Yet, student writing is still primarily evaluated based on single-authored products like essays. Even so, MOOs offer new (and increasingly credible) modes of collaboration that are instrumental in redefining what it means to collaborate.

Why Collaborate Using MOOs?

In the past twenty years or so, educators have come to realize that students learn quickly and in comprehensive ways by writing. E. M. Forster said, "I never know what I think until I see what I have written." In other words, we learn what we think by writing. Where better to do so than in a MOO where writing constitutes the entire MOOscape! So, if collaboration improves learning, as we suggest, and if writing is a way of learning, then using a MOO for writing together (whether talking or coauthoring) is one of the most important reasons to collaborate on a MOO.

Building a community is another reason to use MOOs as collaborative environments. When you enter a MOO, you enter a community. If you have your own player account, your creations (your room and other objects) contribute to the community. These creations are written into the community in your name (as objects you own), but the entire process of building the community is collaborative because (as we explained in Chapter 1) a MOO is a user-extendable program. Most public or semi-public MOOs will have a building policy that you should read before creating objects or rooms. It is also advisable to explore some of the other MOO citizens' rooms to get ideas for designing your own (provided you ask permission first). The community is, in some sense, the sum of its users and their writing, and is subject to comments and criticisms where needed. For example, recently a guest logged on to Lingua MOO and wrote us a MOOmail about our use of ASCII graphic maps in some areas of the MOO. The problem was that she is blind and uses a computerized voice synthesizer and speech recognition system in order to "read" the MOO screens and speak commands in order to be translated into text. The ASCII graphics were wreaking havoc when she entered a space that used a map to show a 3-D rendering of the area. What she heard was a lot of text characters being read (like slash, slash, underscore, period, etc.), which did her no good in terms of knowing what kind of space she was in, much less where to go and how. We thanked her for her comments and added a line to our welcome screen that instructs users how to turn the ASCII graphics off when they log on. This is just one way that our community has been improved by a collaborative moment at Lingua MOO.

Another reason for collaborating on a MOO is to increase your self-confidence in writing and thinking. Too often the opportunity to try out an idea or speak your opinion about something in class is rare or cut short by class time limitations. Furthermore, the dynamics of the class (including the teacher and other student personalities) may not make you feel inclined to speak up in class. We have found that students mention this problem as one of the most positive aspects about using a MOO. One student wrote:

> I feel it encourages more discussion, maybe it sometimes encourages more frivolous discussions, but that can be stopped by the other team members. I think people felt more at ease online than they might face to face with someone they don't know that well. There might be some security in a little distance between participants.

When asked if using the MOO improved their writing, another student wrote:

> Yes, my improvement was a direct result of the opportunity it provided to speak out (sometimes totally against everyone else) at times when I would not have attempted to do so. It was like unraveling some fear of speaking that was holding me hostage.

You may even find that when class is over students often make plans to continue their discussion at the MOO later. As we have emphasized in several ways, the MOO allows you to break the traditional boundaries of time and space, and even what constitutes the meaning of a "class," by enabling you to redefine class time and class work. This is not to say that your class will begin to meet during times not scheduled in your syllabus, but only that it is *possible* for students and teachers to extend the accessibility they have to one another by meeting at the MOO at unscheduled times (when desired). This possibility and whether you take advantage of it is entirely up to you, and may depend on whether you have access to a computer with Internet connectivity outside of class time. But increasing numbers of schools are installing networks and computer labs that radically supplement what traditional education has offered in the past—a typical classroom limited to X number of students who must meet for X number of hours.

One effect of the MOO's capability of extending class in terms of time and space is also the ability for a given class to meet with other classes from other locations in real-time. MOO teleseminars, as they are sometimes called, take collaboration to a new level. Not only will the MOO facilitate collaboration among your classmates, but now you can work with other students from other towns, other states, even other countries. Whole networks of teachers who use MOOs are springing up, making it possible for teachers with similar courses to locate each other and actually coordinate collaboration by assigning team projects, meeting as one large class in real-time, and other innovative and creative ways of joining forces toward similar educational goals. The question you may be asking is WHY do this?

It is not so much because students may meet interesting people from other cultures (though this has its own benefits), but because these meetings often introduce new modes of collaboration that encourage students to learn to view things from new perspectives, as well as to serve as real audiences for one another. Unlike traditional writing assignments in which individual students must contrive or fictionalize an audience for their writing, collaboration among groups of classes, especially from diverse cultures, creates the possibility for writing that is timely, relevant, more real, and more dynamic.

In addition, such collaborations encourage the sharing of resources. What one student in one class can reasonably be expected to gather in the way of research sources is exponentially increased when allowed to collaborate with students in other classes. The trick is to understand the implications of sharing resources (and/or writing) that could result in plagiarism.

Plagiarism is a serious academic offense, and in no way are we suggesting that collaboration on MOOs will result in plagiarism. Nor should you assume that you need to be overly cautious and worry that other students (either in your own class or one with which your class is collaborating) will take advantage of your generosity in sharing resources and ideas. If you suspect someone is taking advantage of a collaborative situation, you should notify your teacher before confronting him or her.

How to Collaborate on MOOs

Now that we have broadened the definition of collaboration to include working relationships on the MOO, and we have listed some of the most important reasons for collaboration on MOOs, we turn now to some important tips on and examples of how to collaborate in MOOspace.[1]

Much depends, of course, on the occasion for establishing a collaborative working relationship on the MOO, but let's assume that you have an assignment in a writing class that calls for a group project among your own classmates. Say that your group must meet on the MOO and write a policy on distance education for your school. First, the group should determine some possible times outside of class to meet at the MOO, and you should make sure all members of the group have access to the MOO at those times. It would be helpful to set up a schedule of meetings, and perhaps the first meeting could lay out the project and some defining goals and tasks.

As with any group project, it is important to balance the tasks among the members of the group fairly and define the tasks clearly. Be sure to record your meetings from the start, and it would be useful to create a $container in your meeting place at the MOO for putting $notes relating to the policy document and for MOO equipment that you will be using (such as MOO Slides, Project Boards, and so forth). If necessary, whoever creates and owns the $notes may want to encrypt them so that only group members can read them. Some MOOs may also make it possible for multiple ownership of the evolving document so that more than the owner of the $note may edit it. You should check with the MOO administrators to see if this is possible.

Another important practice to establish from the start is a communication system among the members of the group so that between MOO sessions questions and comments can circulate. We recommend that you see if the MOO administrators will set up an inMOO mailing list for your group, one that you can each subscribe to so that whenever anyone posts to the list, just as on an e-mail listserv, all subscribers receive the post. It also centralizes the posts so that if one person's e-mail provider goes down temporarily, they don't lose communications from the group. Chances are that everyone will still have access to Telnet to the MOO and check their MOOmail.

As we suggested, early MOO sessions should focus on a timeline and working list of tasks for how the policy document will take shape. If interviews are required, these can easily be conducted at the MOO, especially if you are interviewing people who do not live in your city. You can send them instructions for logging on to the MOO and the basic commands by e-mail or fax, and you can record the interview and $notedit it later, if necessary, to retain only the portions relevant to your developing policy on distance education. The fact that you write such a policy using distance education technology should also work in your favor, and gives the policy extra credibility.

$$\textcircled{!}$$

If, as part of your research, you conduct interviews on a MOO (or by e-mail for that matter), make sure that you obtain permission from your source to quote them in your paper or project, noting the exact date and time of the interview in your works cited. If you record the interview in the MOO, that information is automatically included in the heading of the tape.

In addition to MOO sessions where you discuss the project, you might also consider using Netscape and the enCore Xpress MOO client for group WWW surfing, using your MOO window to discuss Web sites that you all see in your Web browser windows, and swapping URL addresses and book-marking key sites to include in your research as you go. If you are using enCore Xpress you can use the @url command at any time (Figure 9.1) to display a Web page to your collaborative partners.

Once your group has sufficient research, it is time to begin drafting the policy. There are a number of ways this can occur. You can either use asynchronous MOOmails back and forth, synchronous MOO sessions, or a combination of both. For example, if you find it hard to get started on the actual writing, have the group meet online together, turn on a recorder and just start talking through the paper. Each group member will contribute ideas about how to structure the document and how to introduce it, and so forth. As you talk on the MOO, recording as you go, keep in mind that just as in any writing project you do on your own, the sequence of writing down the ideas is not so important in the beginning so much as getting it all down. The beauty of the recorded group MOO session (and this works for two or more people working) is that once you end the session and turn the recorder off, you have the basic stuff in the form of a conversation. Now you can take a number of different paths to completion.

Each group member may want to e-mail themselves a copy of the log in order to reread it later and make notes about things to add or delete. Working by MOOmail, the group members may want to communicate with a designated member who will take these comments and filter out any repetition

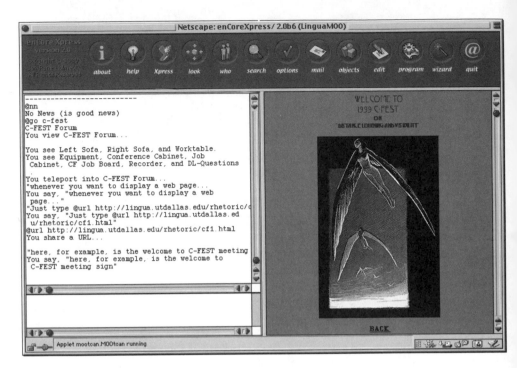

FIGURE 9.1   The @url Command

among the comments, and sequence them according to the earlier identified structure of the document. Another group member, possibly the owner of the logged session $note, may then start the process of eliminating all the conversational cues in the log (all the *Cynthia says, Jan says, Jan smiles, Cynthia thinks*, etc.), retaining just the portions of the text that can be shaped into sentences, paragraphs, and sections. As the document takes shape, subsequent MOO meetings can focus on further refinement of the text until the final product is ready for proofreading. Once it is finished, it is possible to e-mail the $note/document to anyone, including your teacher. Or, if you are required to hand in a hard copy of it, it's easy to read the $note while on the MOO and copy and paste it into a word file. If the MOO you work on is an enCore MOO, then the $note is actually also a Web page because the Web interface makes of every object in the MOO (including $notes) a Web page complete with the background template and word wrapping. And how appropriate for a policy on distance education to be turned in as a URL address or a MOO $note! Imagine e-mailing your teacher with one line: Distance Education Policy by (group names here) located on the WWW at:

http://someserver.someschool.edu:7000/obj#

Let's say that you are assigned to collaborate with some students from another class located somewhere else in the world, students that you meet only on the MOO. The basic tips we listed above for intraclass group projects also apply to these kinds of interclass projects, with some added guidelines.

In addition to setting out clearly defined and equally balanced tasks and goals for the project, you may want to focus in the first few MOO sessions on getting to know each other. Because you only have the MOO persona by which to relate to one another, and may even be from different cultures, it is even more important to establish a sense of your group dynamics and individual styles early on.

Special Case: Language Learning and ESL / FL

Recently, a new application of collaboration on MOOs has emerged in the language learning fields. Computer-assisted language learning (CALL) has been around for a few years, but mostly this consisted of skill-and-drill type computer software. Now, MOOs are making it possible for language learners to meet in real-time and talk to native speakers of the target language.

(i)

If you would like to learn/practice your language skills in any of the languages of the following MOOs, we strongly encourage you to visit them and talk to the players online. Some of the educational language learning MOOs currently open for student access are schMOOze (ESL), MUNDO Hispano (Spanish), Little Italy (Italian), and Dreistadt MOO (German).[2]

Methods of collaboration in language learning range from simple open assignments to more dedicated pairing like "tandem learning." In the first case, students are often assigned to visit the language MOO, having to read all room and object descriptions in the target language, communicating in the language by typing the commands in that language, talking spontaneously with native speakers, and exploring the MOO by moving around, again having to use commands in the target language in order to do so. Tandem learning involves a team of two language learners, each experts in their native language and learners of the other's native language. The idea is that being simultaneously an expert and a learner enriches and facilitates the language learning process in new ways.

Language acquisition experts agree that text-based approaches that immerse students in the target language often speed up the process of learning the language, and foreign language and English as a Second Language faculty are swiftly becoming new converts to teaching with MOOs as they realize how such collaborative language learning adds a new and powerful dimension to teaching and learning previously unavailable to them and their students.

A few final words on MOO collaboration. Some of the most unexpected benefits of collaboration on the MOO are the synergy that it creates and the serendipitous relationships that often form online. You never know who you might meet and form a working relationship with, one that may spawn projects that develop from previous collaborations. Such relationships often lead to much more than just thinking in new ways. They can, and have, led to career changes, relocations, book contracts, the formation of new communities (both online and off), and the establishment of new and lasting friendships. Writing may lead you into new domains, but collaboration leads you into new lives.

NOTES

1. For a brief look at how collaboration can work online, take a look at a presentation that we wrote for the 1995 Modern Language Association Conference in Chicago. Not only did we write the piece while online at the MOO, it is *about* collaboration as well. The title is "Synchroni/CITY: Online Collaboration, Research, and Teaching in MOOspace," and it is a good example of a *cyphertext* and how one publishes within the MOO itself. You can find it on the WWW at:

   http://lingua.utdallas.edu:7000/748

2. There are several other foreign language MOOs at this writing, and they may welcome student users; but they did not grant permission to list them here. We recommend that if you locate one you wish to visit, you e-mail the administrators to request permission for you and/or your class to visit.

CLASS DISCUSSION

1. Discuss similarities of and differences between plagiarism and collaboration. What kinds of projects have you collaborated on before? Were they graded as a group or individually? In general, how do you feel about collaborating on writing assignments? Do you think the MOO makes collaboration easier or more difficult?

2. What is "intellectual property" and what are the boundaries of copyright in electronic communities like educational MOOs (and/or Web pages published in a MOO)? Optional reading for class discussion: John Perry Barlow's article on intellectual property first published in *WIRED* magazine, available at:

   http://www.wired.com/wired/2.03/features/economy.ideas.html

3. Visit some of the language learning MOOs listed below (you will need to use Telnet or your MOO client to reach them at the addresses below) and discuss language learning in MOOs in terms of foreign languages and English as a Second Language.

```
Dreistadt (German)         -- cmc.uib.no 7777
Little Italy (Italian)     -- littleitaly.moo.mud.org 4444
MundoHispano (Spanish)     -- moo.syr.edu 8888
schMOOze University (ESL)  -- schmooze.hunter.cuny.edu 8888
```

EXERCISES

1. Design a collaboative MOO project proposal that involves two or more students in your class. You can think in terms of staging a play and videotaping it online, or another kind of MOO event like a poetry reading or panel discussion. The key is to design the project, conceive it, and write it up from beginning to end.

2. Create the project's necessary MOO equipment and containers. Create a project board to track the progress of the project and list the tasks by name.

3. After the project is over, write up a description of the project, the results, and experiences you learned.

APPENDIX A

Quick Reference to MOO Commands

Below is a list of commands and verbs that are available in MOOs that are built on the LambdaCore and enCore databases. Most of these commands are well documented in the MOO's online help system. To get help, or find out more about a certain command or topic, type *help command/topic* at any time while logged on to the MOO. For example, to read more about the *@who* command and how to use it, type:

```
help @who
```

To start exploring the help system, you can also simply type *help* for an overview of topics for which further information can be provided. Learn to use the online help system effectively; it will save you lots of time and frustration later.

General MOO Commands and Help Topics

name	communication	full-index	inventory
"	decrypt	@gag	@lastlog
:	delete	gagging	letters
::	@describe	@gaglist	@linelength
?	descriptions	gen-index	@listgag
@add-alias	drop	@gender	look
@add-feature	@edit	get	manipulation
@addalias	@edit-options	give	manners
@addfeature	@editoptions	go	@memory
@age	editors	gopher	messages
alias	@eject	@gripe	@messages
aliases	@eject!	hand	miscellaneous
backspace	cmote	help	@mode
@bug	encrypt	home	@more
burn	erase	@idea	@move
@check	examine	index	movement
@check-full	@examine	information	news
commands	features	insert	@notedit
@comment	@features	introduction	notes

157

objects	put	@sethome	@users
options	@quit	spivak	@version
output	read	spoofing	whereis
page	@registerme	@suggest	whisper
@pagelength	remove	summary	@who
@paranoid	@remove-feature	@sweep	wizard-list
@password	@rename	take	wizard-names
player-names	@request-	throw	@wrap
players	character	tinymud	write
privacy	@rmalias	@typo	
programming	say	@ungag	
pronouns	security	@uptime	

MOOmail-Specific Commands and Help Topics

@add-notify	mail-index	@qsend	@rn
@answer	@mail-options	@quickreply	@send
@copymail	@mailoptions	@quicksend	@skip
@forward	message-	@read	@subscribe
@keep-mail	sequences	@read-all-new-	@subscribed
@keepmail	@netforward	mail	@unrmmail
mail	@next	@refile	@unsubscribe
@mail	@nn	@renumber	zombie-messages
@mail-all-new-	@peek	@reply	
mail	@prev	@resend	
mail-forwarding	@qreply	@rmmail	

Commands and Help Topics for Builders

@add-entrance	containers	lock	rooms
@add-exit	@contents	@lock_for_open	@set
@add-owned	@count	locking	@setprop
@audit	@create	@measure	@sort-owned
@build-options	creation	object-quota	thing-messages
builder-index	@dig	@opacity	topology
@builder-options	@dump	@parents	@unlock
@builderoptions	@entrances	@quota	@unlock_for_open
building	exit-messages	@recreate	@verify-owned
@buildoptions	@exits	@recycle	
@classes	key-	@remove-entrance	
common_quota	representation	@remove-exit	
container-	keys	@resident	
messages	@locations	room-messages	

Programmer-Specific Commands

#	@display-options	@list#	@remove-feature
;	@displayoptions	mail	@rename#
@add-alias#	@egrep	options	@rm-alias#
@add-feature	errors	precedence	@rmalias#
@addalias#	eval	prepositions	@rmproperty
@args	examine	prog-index	@rmverb
@args#	expressions	@prog-options	@rmverb#
@check-chparent	features	@progoptions	scattering
@check-property	.flush	@program	@setenv
@chmod	@forked	.program	@show
@chmod#	functions	@program#	statements
@chparent	@grep	@programmer-options	tasks
@clearproperty	help	@programmeroptions	truth
@copy	@kids	programming	utilities
@dbsize	@kill	@property	utils
@disinherit	@killquiet	@prospectus	@verb
@disown	language	regular-	
@display	@list	expressions	

Built-in Programming Functions for Programmers

abs()	create()	listappend()
acos()	crypt()	listdelete()
add_property()	ctime()	listen()
add_verb()	db_disk_size()	listeners()
asin()	decode_binary()	listinsert()
atan()	delete_property()	listset()
binary_hash()	delete_verb()	log()
boot_player()	disassemble()	log10()
buffered_output_	dump_database()	match()
length()	encode_binary()	max()
builtin-index	equal()	max_object()
call_function()	eval()	memory_usage()
caller_perms()	exp()	min()
callers()	floatstr()	move()
ceil()	floor()	notify()
children()	flush_input()	object_bytes()
chparent()	force_input()	open_network_
clear_property()	function_info()	connection()
connected_players()	idle_seconds()	output_delimiters()
connected_seconds()	index()	parent()
connection_name()	is_clear_property()	pass()
connection_option()	is_member()	players()
connection_options()	is_player()	properties()
cos()	kill_task()	property_info()
cosh()	length()	queue_info()

```
queued_tasks()        set_verb_args()       ticks_left()
raise()               set_verb_code()       time()
random()              set_verb_info()       tofloat()
read()                setadd()              toint()
recycle()             setremove()           toliteral()
renumber()            shutdown()            tonum()
reset_max_object()    sin()                 toobj()
resume()              sinh()                tostr()
rindex()              sqrt()                trunc()
rmatch()              strcmp()              typeof()
seconds_left()        string_hash()         unlisten()
server_log()          strsub()              valid()
server_version()      substitute()          value_bytes()
set_connection_       suspend()             value_hash()
  option()            tan()                 verb_args()
set_player_flag()     tanh()                verb_code()
set_property_info()   task_id()             verb_info()
set_task_perms()      task_stack()          verbs()
```

General MOO Core-Specific Help Topics

```
$big_mail_         $guest_log         $room             MR-expiration
  recipient        $help              $webslate_utils   MR-naming
$biglist           $housekeeper       core-index        MR-reading
$container         $login             mail-expiration   MR-searching
$error             $mail_agent        mail-format       MR-sequences
$exit              $mail_recipient    mail-resolution   MR-subscribing
$generic_db        $news              mail-resolve      MR-writing
$generic_editor    $no_one            mail-system       object-matching
$generic_help      $player_db         matching          receiving-mail
$generic_options   $recycler          MR-access         sending-mail
```

APPENDIX B

Glossary of MOO Jargon and Acronyms

@ symbol   Special character used to denote commands that interact with the MOO system rather than the virtual reality of the MOOspace. Examples include @*who* (used to see who is online), @*quit* (used to disconnect from the MOO). Commands without the @ *symbol*, such as *look*, are used to interact with the virtual reality of the MOOspace.

$ symbol   Used to denote objects that are integral parts of the MOO core. These objects are defined on the system object (#0) and are the essential building blocks in the MOO. Instead of using object numbers, we refer to these objects using the $-sign. For example, the generic thing which has object number #5 can also be referred to as $thing as in the command @*create $thing named Book*.

afk   Away from keyboard.

alias   All MOO objects (including players) may have aliases used primarily as shortcuts to typing the full object name.

argument   The specified syntax of the verb being defined. Since the MOO is a text-based, command line oriented system, verbs are usually invoked when someone types a command that executes them (i.e., *read book*). In order to execute the correct verb, the MOO needs to know on what object it is defined (the direct object) and whether or not a preposition or an indirect object is allowed as part of the command syntax (for example, in the command *put book in shelf*). Learning to program in MOO involves learning how verbs are defined and arguments are specified.

bot   An object designed to interact in real time with MOO users in its vicinity. The bot (short for robot) consists of a series of programs that interpret and act on conversation and sentence patterns through random responses or question responses, all of which are user programmable. The most common bot in enCore-based Moos was designed by Ken Schweller of CollegeTown MOO, but a number of other types of bots can also be encountered in MOOs, including bots that can "walk" from location to location, and bots that can "learn" and "remember" from their interaction with users. Bots require more advanced building and programming skills, but can be used creatively for tutorials, dramas, or presentation of research, among other things.

brb   Be right back.

btw   By the way.

builder   A type of player who can create new rooms and other objects in the MOO. In order to use the building features the MOO has to offer, your character must be a builder. If you don't have builder status, request it from a MOO administrator.

building   The process by which players in a MOO add new spaces in the form of rooms or other types of objects. The most common building commands are @*dig* and @*create,* which make new rooms and objects.

client   A special software program used to access a MOO.

commands   Special MOO programs for interacting with the MOO system.

emote/emoticon   A type of action, emotion, or smiley face written by players in order to express emotion, represent an action they are doing, or punctuate what they say with a smiley face :-).

enCore   An educational MOO designed to be used as a basis for new MOOs.

F2F   Face-to-face.

generics   Also known as a class. This is used to describe a set of objects that inherit the same set of characteristics, such as properties and verbs. See **object.**

guests   Special player class designated for visitors to the MOO. Guests do not need a password to access a MOO.

host   A computer that runs a MOO or other applications.

IMHO   In my humble opinion.

IRL   In real life.

lag   When the Internet or the MOO causes you to stop receiving input or sending output to the MOO (usually temporary, lasting from a few seconds to sometimes minutes depending on where the problem lies).

LambdaMOO   The first MOO, started by Pavel Curtis in 1990. Still one of the biggest and most populated virtual spaces on the Internet.

LOL   Laughing out loud.

MOO   Multi-User Domain Object-Oriented.

MUD   Multi-User Dungeon or Domain.

newbie   New or inexperienced MOO user.

object   The basic element in the MOO universe. An object is a collection of MOO programs/commands and properties/data that define the object.

object-oriented programming (OOP)   Paradigm in computer science that provides a way to conceptualize and implement programs on a computer.

players   Users in a MOO who belong to a hierarchy of player classes, each of which define certain attributes and available options. Generic player classes are: guest, player, builder, programmer, wizard.

programmer   A type of player who can use the MOO's internal programming language to alter the functionality of the MOO itself. Programmers are also builders by default. Being a programmer is a privilege that will empower you with tools to create much more elaborate and interactive objects than you could as a builder. With the MOO programming language you can program almost anything you want. Along with this privilege, however, goes a responsibility. Therefore, many MOOs will only give "programmer bits" if you commit to their policies on programming.

property   A slot on an object that is used to store data or characteristics about the object.

RL   Real life.

ROFL   Rolling on the floor laughing.

server   A program that runs a MOO database; can also mean a computer that runs a MOO. See **host.**

syntax   The MOO language grammar. In order for the MOO to understand the commands that you write, the commands must adhere to a very strict syntax, which is defined in the MOO language. At the simplest level, the syntax of MOO commands requires you to name both an object and an action associated with that object when you want to interact with the object. For example, if you come across a pot of hot coffee, and you want to drink the coffee, you must type a command such as *drink coffee.* In this case, *drink* refers to the action you can perform on the object named *coffee.* At a deeper level, syntax refers to the format in which MOO programs must be written in order to be understood by the MOO system. This syntax is defined through the MOO's internal programming language, and must be followed strictly by programmers who wish to write MOO programs.

teleport   Method for moving quickly between two locations/rooms in a MOO. Teleport commands include *@go* and *@join.*

TTYL   Talk to you later.

verb   A MOO computer program or algorithm describing in detail how the computer should solve a given problem.

VR   Virtual reality.

wizard   MOO administrator.

world   MOOs are often called *worlds* in many MOO client programs.

APPENDIX C

A Few Educational MOOs*

Achieve: Collaborative Virtual Learning @ Schoolnet
WWW: http://achieve.utoronto.ca/

AppalachiaMOO (enCore based)
Telnet: ariel.clc.wvu.edu 7777
WWW: http://www.clc.wvu.edu

ArkMOO (enCore-based)
Telnet: pathos.rhet.ualr.edu 8888
WWW: http://pathos.rhet.ualr.edu:7000/

ATHEMOO
Telnet: moo.hawaii.edu 9999
WWW: http://moo.hawaii.edu:7000/

AtlantisMOO
Telnet: Atlantis.fe.up.pt 7777
WWW: http://Atlantis.fe.up.pt

AussieMOO
Telnet: farrer.riv.csu.edu.au 7777
WWW: http://farrer.riv.csu.edu.au/aussiemoo.html

BioMOO, Virtual meeting place for biologists
Telnet: bioinfo.weizmann.ac.il 8888
WWW: http://bioinfo.weizmann.ac.il/BioMOO

CaraMOO (enCore based)
Telnet: moo.adultedu.gla.ac.uk 7777
WWW: http://www.adultedu.gla.ac.uk:7000

---

*Note: These sites have agreed to being listed in this Appendix, and they were online as of October 24, 1999. We cannot, however, guarantee that they will not change.

CivicMOO (enCore based)
Telnet: wonka.tincan.org 7777
WWW: http://www.tincan.org/~voices

CollegeTown MOO
Telnet: ctown.bvu.edu 7777
WWW: http://www.bvu.edu/ctown

CoMentor
WWW: http://comentor.hud.ac.uk:7000

Connections
Telnet: connections.moo.mud.org 3333
WWW: http://web.nwe.ufl.edu/~tari/connections

DaMOO
Telnet: DaMOO.csun.edu 7777
WWW: http://DaMOO.csun.edu:8888

Diversity University MOO
Telnet: moo.du.org 8888 (or 128.18.101.106 8888)
WWW: http://moo.du.org:8000

Dreistadt (enCore-based)
Telnet: cmc.uib.no 7777
WWW: http://cmc.uib.no:7001

EdMOO
WWW: http://edx3.educ.monash.edu.au/edmoo/

GrassRoots MOO
Telnet: health.acor.org 8888
WWW: http://www.enabling.org/grassroots/

Isle of the Net (enCore-based)
Telnet: maryann.hu.mtu.edu 8888
WWW: http://www.hu.mtu.edu:7000

Lingua MOO (enCore-based)
Telnet: lingua.utdallas.edu 8888
WWW: http://lingua.utdallas.edu:7000

Little Italy
Telnet: littleitaly.moo.mud.org 4444
WWW: http://little.usr.dsi.unimi.it:8888

The Mediatrix
Telnet: moo.lib.uiowa.edu 7777
WWW: http://moo.lib.uiowa.edu

Meridian MOO
Telnet: sky.bellcore.com 7777

MOOkti: A Polysynchronous Learning Environment for Graduate Education
WWW: http://noisey.oise.utoronto.ca:9996

MOOscape (enCore-based)
Telnet: scape.uta.edu 7777

MOOSE Crossing
Telnet: moose-crossing.cc.gatech.edu 7777

MOOville
Telnet: moo.nwe.ufl.edu 9898
WWW: http://web.nwe.ufl.edu/writing/help/moo

MooWP
Telnet: moo.uwp.edu 7777
WWW: http://moo.uwp.edu:8000

MundoHispano
Telnet: admiral.umsl.edu 8888
WWW: http://www.umsl.edu/~moosproj/mundo.html

OldPuebloMOO (encore-based)
Telnet: 128.196.59.16 7777
WWW: http://www.fcii.arizona.edu/oldpueblomoo/

ROO MOO
Telnet: saga.umkc.edu 4444
WWW: http://iml.umkc.edu/roo/

schMOOze University
Telnet: schmooze.hunter.cuny.edu 8888
WWW: http://schmooze.hunter.cuny.edu:8888

SCIENCEMOO

Telnet: flourish.mrl.nyu.edu:8888

WWW: http://flourish.mrl.nyu.edu:8000/

The Solar System Simulation

Telnet: solsys.eou.edu 4567

WWW: http://www.solsys.eou.edu/~solsys

(formerly the NAU Solar System Simulation 1990–1998. Note: This online social and communications sciences laboratory requires preregistration for admission; consult SolSySim Homepage http://www.nau.edu/anthro/solsys.)

TAPPED IN

Telnet: moo.tappedin.sri.com 7777

WWW: http://www.tappedin.org/

TECFAMOO

Telnet: tecfamoo.unige.ch 7777

WWW: http://tecfa.unige.ch/moo/tecfamoo.html

UWM MOO (enCore based)

Telnet: www.uwm.edu 7777

WWW: http://www.uwm.edu:7000

Virtual Campus

Telnet: moo.arch.usyd.edu.au 7777

WWW: http://moo.arch.usyd.edu.au:7778

The Virtual Writing Center MOO (VWCMOO)

Telnet: bessie.englab.slcc.edu 7777

WWW: http://bessie.englab.slcc.edu:7777/

Walden3 MOO (enCore based)

Telnet: walden3.mhpcc.edu 8888

WWW: http://walden3.mhpccc.edu/moo/

ZooMOO

Telnet: moo.missouri.edu 8888

WWW: http://moo.missouri.edu/

INDEX